MOVE FORWARD

A Guide to Having the Life you Want

By: Lani Nelson Zlupko, Ph.D., LCSW

LNZ | Consulting
Move forward with Career, Family, Life
P.O. Box 8028
Wilmington, DE 19803
302.543.6296
Lani@LNZconsulting.com
www.LNZconsulting.com

introduction

INTRODUCTION: WHAT CAN MOVE FORWARD DO FOR ME?

Life is great, but not all the time. People are wonderful, but not in all ways. When life gets complicated, and relationships are problematic, the MOVE Forward approach helps you:

- Move past a troubling event, crisis, or relationship
- Strengthen existing relationships
- Resolve a difficult issue
- Manage a major transition in your life
- Gain traction in places where you feel stuck

A challenge may arise in the form of a personal tragedy, a relationship problem, a career crisis, or simply the hazards of normal living, in which old rules of operating no longer work.

As a therapist, researcher, and consultant specializing in transition management, I have had over twenty years' experience helping people manage difficult situations, reinvent themselves, and move forward in their careers and personal lives with a more evolved sense of self. I developed MOVE Forward to help people achieve mastery in confronting challenges.

MOVE Forward is **skill-based.** You will learn skills that enable you to handle problems with emotional integrity, instead of being hijacked by them. Even more, you will learn to transform and evolve into a more composed, empowered, skillful version of yourself. You will gain mastery over your emotions and reactions, which enhances your ability to direct your life. You will learn to "Start your day happy, end your day happy," no matter what comes your way.

MOVE Forward moves you from your current mode of being to a new mode:

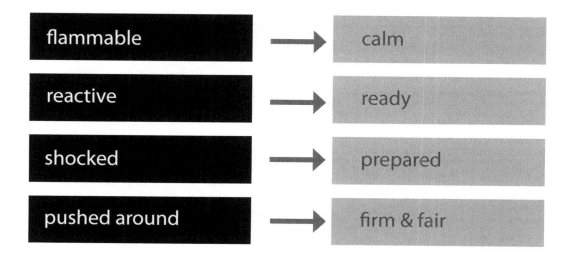

This workbook takes you through the process of working through your challenges, whatever they may be. After describing the basic MOVE Forward principles, the workbook will guide you through applying them in your own life. MOVE Forward consists of 4 steps, and you will be taken through all of them:

····▶ **M**ove Back from emotional drama and chaos.

····▶ **O**bserve what is happening clearly and candidly.

····▶ **V**isualize a better way.

····▶ **E**volve into someone who is poised, Skilled Up, and ready to move forward.

Each step includes several specific strategies and is illustrated by a number of scenarios—examples of challenges people commonly face.

Here Are Some Sample Scenarios:

✓ You have high goals for yourself, but the needs of your kids, co-workers, and family members keep getting in your way.
How can you remain caring yet still move forward?

✓ Your spouse is a decent person, but has habits that grind your nerves. You're afraid that mentioning "petty issues" might harm your marriage, but saying nothing isn't working either.
How can you address these issues while improving your relationship?

✓ You experienced a traumatic event as a young adult. You feel that enough years have passed and you should be "over it" by now. You've tried many approaches, but negative emotions still linger.
How can you resolve this issue for good?

✓ You share office space with an annoying co-worker. You are reliable; that person chronically under-performs.
How can you de-link your sanity and your reputation from this person without seeming callous, mean-spirited, or unprofessional?

✓ You have suffered through a horrible long-term relationship with a spouse or a parent. It has left you feeling scarred and un-whole.
How can you learn to feel hopeful and optimistic again?

✓ Your company is laying off people right and left. It is a scary time to be left standing. You can't help but think, "Am I next?"
How can you learn to remain confident in this environment?

✓ You love your son. You don't want to yell at him; he deserves better. But try as you might, you find yourself screaming at full throttle, saying things you wouldn't dare say to a stranger.
How can you learn to keep this relationship loving, open, and intact?

skill gap

Skill Gap is a basic MOVE Forward principle. It asks us to re-interpret our own and others' negative actions as being caused by a lack of skills rather than a permanent flaw or personal failing. In our society, it is very tempting to label people as weak or permanently damaged. We often believe, mistakenly, that our problems will always remain a part of us. For example, when people say, "I'm an anxious person," or "My family has always been depressed," they are suggesting that there is no hope for change.

While a clear, candid assessment of ourselves and others is essential (see Step 2, Observe), it is also important to understand that many of our problems can and do resolve when we apply new skills to them. A new approach can literally transform our behavior patterns, our feelings, and the neurochemical effects of negative emotions in our body. Stress is often just the result of living with a skill set that is outdated or inadequate for current needs and challenges.

Modern research simply does not support the idea that people cannot change. Actually, research demonstrates time and again that when we give people new ways of coping and interacting—new skills—they can evolve in vital ways. While some people do remain inflexible, most are remarkably resilient and capable of profound change.

Consider These Examples of Different Skill Gaps:

▶ A toddler has a meltdown. He's anxious because he lacks the skills to handle too many children crowding him in the sandbox.

▶ A sixth-grader blows up after school because of mounting homework. She lacks the skills to handle the exponentially rising challenges of middle school.

▶ A teenager slams a door, screaming, "You never listen!!" He lacks the skills to say, "I disagree with what you are saying and I want to feel heard."

▶ A spouse throws a glass at her husband when he belittles her. She loses control because she lacks the skills to say, "I won't tolerate you speaking to me time after time that way. Try it again respectfully or I will find another place to stay tonight."

▶ A lawyer who lost her court case sinks into a chair later that evening feeling resigned and thinking, "It's no use. I need to find another job." She would benefit from two skills: better preparing her arguments to match the skill level of her opponents; and reframing a loss as an opportunity for future growth.

Interpreting other people's shortcomings and our own as the result of a Skill Gap is a more accurate and often much more productive way to begin applying new skills to the problems we encounter in life.

> **BUT WAIT!**

What do you mean, "Start my day happy, end my day happy? Are you suggesting I tolerate abusive people and situations?

No. No one should ever tolerate abusive people or situations. MOVE Forward will help you discern when something is happening that you do not like, and when and how you can protect yourself and take proper action.

Are you suggesting that I'm the problem? Isn't my problem them? What if I didn't do anything to cause this situation?

Sometimes you are not the cause of the problem. But it is also true that you can control your reaction to it. That is something you can begin to change now. How do I know this? Try this experiment. Imagine that person walking out the door. Problem solved? Or are you still fuming and rattled, even after they're gone? Many people find that problem relationships and dynamics repeat themselves until they are fully and effectively equipped with the skills to address them.

What if I am the problem? What if this problem exists because of me?

Sometimes decisions we made in the past are regrettable. Today, we have a choice: do we want to forever live with regret and self-punishment over mistakes, or do we believe that like everyone else, we deserve the chance to mature, evolve, and grow into a better version of ourselves?

Interestingly, most people agree that they should give others a chance to grow and improve. Our children or our friends deserve that, right? Yet we sometimes hold ourselves to impossible standards: "I wasn't perfect then, and I must pay for it forever."

If you want to move on, you must be prepared to let yourself off the hook for being imperfect in your earlier years or even yesterday. You must believe that you can start the next chapter of your life today. If you feel you are the problem, consider thinking of it this way: you were imperfect and had some Skilling Up to do. Welcome to the human race. We all do.

BUT WAIT!

Will I need to go back and relive unhappy events?

No. Not entirely. Rehashing, it turns out, can reinforce the feeling of being stuck. You will use your difficult past events to identify problem zones, then load up on new skills for navigating these areas. You will not remain stuck; you will not become hopeless, and you will not blame yourself or anyone else for your prior flaws. You will use these past events as a learning ground for skill development.

Can't I just meditate? Or medicate?

Though meditation is an effective technique for helping people reduce stress, it is often not enough. People need practical, problem-solving skills for encountering difficult situations in "real time." You need to know exactly what to say and do when faced with your challenge; in such a situation, meditation is usually not an option.

The same goes for medication. Medicating can be very effective to treat the symptoms of depression, anxiety, and other distress. However, medication alone does not equip people to manage their lives. In fact, when people take medication without also learning good skill-building they may wind up tolerating bad situations far longer than they should.

MOVE Forward is not a "cure" for depression, anxiety or stress, but it contains tools that are highly effective in relieving these problems. Many clients who came to me with long-standing depression, anxiety, and stress have eliminated their symptoms using the skills you're about to learn.

GOOD ENOUGH–AND GROWING

This brings us to another basic MOVE Forward principle: Good Enough AND Growing. If you are judging yourself harshly, or feeling open to harsh judgments by others, this is a wonderful principle to master.

Good Enough insists you are a decent, worthy person, AND in need of a few more skills in life. Once you arrive here, you are good company for yourself as you move forward. Just as you would for someone you love, give yourself some reassurances:

- You're a great person AND you're seeking a few more skills.

- You're terrific--AND you could use a tuneup.

- You've worked really hard, AND life has gotten more complicated. You could use a few more techniques to manage it, AND you're on your way--starting today!

You're ready to start Skilling Up. Let's move into Step 1: Move Back.

STEP 1

move back

MOVE BACK: WHAT IS IT?

What does it mean to Move Back, and why is that important? When a provocative comment, situation, event, or dynamic triggers us emotionally, our bodies and minds typically react as if we have been attacked. If we do not learn to filter our first response, we are likely to behave in emotionally charged ways that we will regret. We may feel we have exposed too much of ourselves, over-reacted, under-responded, yielded too far, compromised too much, over-promised, lashed back, and so on.

We may also feel assaulted by relentless thoughts: "Why did I do that? How could I have done that? What's wrong with me that I . . .?" Such thoughts keep us from thinking more clearly and positively. When we find ourselves repeatedly caught in this action-regret cycle, we need to learn to add a pause--that is, to Move Back.

Move Back is a concept that allows us to create a healthy emotional distance from someone or something that is provocative. It is not a permanent retreat, but a temporary, self-imposed "time out" that allows us to detach from a trigger for a moment, break a negative or unproductive cycle we do not want to repeat, and ground ourselves in order to find a more intentional, productive response. Moving back does not mean we do not love or care about someone or something; in fact, we most often need this skill with those we love the most!

Moving back from knee-jerk thoughts and reactions gives us time and space to search for a better way of acting, thinking, and feeling that enables us to respond productively to the trigger. Productive responses typically encourage, empower, and protect our interests in a composed, thoughtful way. They reflect our best version of ourselves.

We live in an over-urgent society where things must be done "right now!" Watch the temptation to act instantly on matters that, in fact, are not urgent. Even trauma surgeons, who need to respond rapidly, function best when they are not consumed by feelings of urgency. Rushed decisions can be fatal. Timely but thoughtful ones are often the best. Rushing into a situation, or conversation, we often find ourselves right in the middle of a flare-up we could have avoided. We run toward chaos, thinking we can "fix it," often to find we have just made matters worse. We are better served by pausing and Moving Back.

Here Are Some Sample Move Back Scenarios:

✓ You are repeatedly shocked, caught off guard, and humiliated by comments your boss makes to you in public.
You need to find a way to feel less victimized and wounded by his comments and more protected and prepared for them.

✓ You find yourself repeating the same argument with your teenage daughter, even though you promised yourself you were not going to have it again!
You know you must figure out how to stop this pattern and learn a new way to talk with her.

✓ You notice that at weekly meetings, a coworker who gets very fired up triggers you to get worked up, too. You don't have the extra emotional energy to spend on such feelings, so you are tempted to avoid these meetings. Yet missing them would hurt you professionally.
You need to be able to attend the meetings without getting pulled in to other people's emotional chaos.

BUT WAIT!

 Shouldn't I let it all "hang loose" with people I am close to? Isn't the first thought that comes to mind the most honest or real one?

If what you are asking is, "Shouldn't I tell my wife to kiss off when she upsets me?" or "Shouldn't I tell my boss I'm furious when she assigns me another ridiculous task?" or "Shouldn't I be able to call myself an idiot when I act like one?"—well, no. I don't recommend any of those. Research suggests that the first thought or words that come to mind are often clouded by misinterpretation, subject to personal insecurities, and full of logical errors. Experience shows that by Moving Back from a first thought we may actually discover a truer, more authentic, more productive thought that better conveys our highest wishes, priorities, and goals.

Here are some specific strategies to help you MOVE BACK.

STRATEGIES

1 Pause: Buy Yourself Some Time

Add a Pause to almost all your responses, whether verbal, email, phone, or anything else. This is an extremely important step for all of us wishing to be more intentional, composed, thoughtful, and in control of our emotions and life. Buy yourself some time--even a second helps, though a few minutes is better and a day or week still better--to respond in the way that best serves you and makes you most proud of yourself. In fact, learning to Pause is what makes all the other steps possible.

Here's How it Works

▶ Routinely screen your phone calls. This buys you time to decide whether you are in the right frame of mind to deal with that other person. If you need to respond right away, you can acknowledge the call with a classy delay such as, "I received your call. I will get back to you this afternoon."

▶ Always *Pause* before responding to emails. Consider answering them at a regular, set time of day, rather than rushing or tucking responses in all day long. Again, if a quick response is useful, consider, "I will be responding to all emails after 4 p.m. Thank you."

▶ Sit on your hands while reading a highly charged email. Do not respond until you feel calm. At that point, answer only, "I will give your email careful consideration and get back to you (tomorrow, Thursday at 4 p.m., after all necessary parties have been consulted, when I have given it due diligence, after I have consulted my home calendar)."

▶ After an unexpected or provocative comment: "Hmmm, let me give that some thought. I'll get back to you."

▶ After an urgent or demanding request: "I need to check my calendar and get back to you."

STRATEGIES

▶ After a particularly challenging comment or "fish hook" of a proposal: "That deserves my highest attention. I'll be able to give it that (specify when)."

▶ When you have a provocative thought such as, "I don't like that about myself" or "Why is everyone else so happy here?" pause and allow for the possibility that this is just a first, knee-jerk thought that might not be accurate or productive. Say to yourself, "Is that thought accurate? Could there be another way of looking at this?"

2 Find Your Center

When we respond to a trigger, we are allowing someone or something to hijack our emotions. It is our duty to protect and moderate our emotions so that we are responsible and poised. We do this by creating and maintaining a clear, calm center. Calm cannot always come from the outside; most often it does not. When there is no calm around us, we can and must create and sustain our own sense of inner calm. In other words, we remain mature, responsible and adult. When we lack the skill of owning and protecting our inner calm, we are perpetual emotional victims, pulled into chaos by others.

When we find ourselves provoked, surprised, or caught off guard, it is essential to Find Our Center in the midst of all our emotions before responding to others. We can't always control when, if, and how we get emotionally hijacked, but we absolutely must gain control over how quickly and masterfully we return to Center.

STRATEGIES

What is a center? What does it feel and look like?

• Some people picture soothing sounds or words, such as "peace"—a sort of meditation in the moment.

• Others experience their center as an inner wisdom, voice, or knowledge that they guard carefully, like a light in a castle. When they hear the sound of their own inner voice, the noise or threats from other people's voices do not drown out their own feelings, choices, and wishes.

• Still others picture a center axle that remains steady as wheels spin around it in multiple directions.

Whatever form your own center takes, it is your responsibility to cultivate it and have it at the ready. It is no one else's duty to give you a center; nor can you blame someone else entirely for "taking it away." They can try; but it is yours to create and protect.

Here's How it Works

▶ He is provoking me, and I feel like screaming. Where is my center? Breathe in, breathe out. I am in charge of my reaction, and I choose calm and poised.

▶ She is in a bad mood. She wants to vent all her troubles to me. I do care, but I don't feel like becoming sour today. I will listen to her talk while I keep my center peaceful.

3 Don't Go on the Ride

Look around. People are worked up. There is a lot of unnecessary excess drama all around us. It is unprofessional, unproductive, and toxic to those seeking steady, intentional living.

STRATEGIES

Many people are "on a ride" of one kind or another. A co-worker may be worked up over a new rule at work. A parent at the bus stop may be mad at the new principal of the school. A parent on the sidelines at the soccer game may be irate over the coach's inaction. On any given day, any of us could go on innumerable rides, but we all have a limited amount of psychic energy. Be alert to the temptation to get pulled onto other people's rides. Don't Go on the Ride. You can "yes" them and "Amen to that" them without actually committing emotionally to their ride.

Here's How it Works

▶ Wow. A coworker just slammed the phone down, exclaiming, "I can't believe what that jerk just said!" You are tempted to find out what happened, but you have several things you simply must finish before the day's end. Choosing not to go on the ride, you say "Hmm!" and nod in agreement but keep your eyes on your computer screen. Or, say, "I hear you" or "You said it." Choose not to give it more emotional investment.

▶ Your toddler flops on the floor in a full-on tantrum. You think to yourself, "She is losing it." You realize she is on a ride that may take some time, and you choose to stay calm so you can help her come down off it when she is ready.

▶ Several parents at your son's high school are furious about a decision a head coach made. They have spent weeks in heated discussion about how wrong it was. You agree. It was wrong. Today, you arrive at the soccer game after a full day of work. You do not feel you have the extra energy for this discussion, and you are not sure it would help anyway. You choose a seat on the far side of the bleachers and pull out a book to read during halftime. For now, you are choosing not to go on the ride.

STRATEGIES

4 ## Let the Daggers Drop

Sometimes we get triggered because someone has actually thrown a verbal dagger at us and insulted us personally or professionally. OUCH!

At these moments it is especially crucial to Move Back, Pause, Find Your Center, and then Let the Daggers Drop. Literally picture the words like daggers falling to the ground, where you can observe them from a healthy emotional distance. If we don't Move Back, the arrows are likely to really pierce us, whether the comment is warranted or not.

"Wow, I can't believe she said that! I am so hurt and offended! She has no right!" Even worse, we stew over the statement or become anxious: "What if she's right? What if I AM no good, or an over-protective mother, or an incompetent employee, too fat, too thin, too ugly..." At other times we become so reactive that we hurl our own dagger back. "Oh yeah? You think I'm ridiculous? How about the way you. . ."

Regrettably, we have now stooped to behavior that is unproductive, hurtful, and does not become us. We have allowed our emotions, time, and energy to be hijacked.

Instead, we can learn to Let the Daggers Drop in the heat of the moment. Later, when we are calm, and in the privacy of our own space, we can always do the necessary candid self-assessment. But during public encounters or in the midst of a rapid phone or email exchange, we are best served by Moving Back, Letting the Daggers Drop, and redirecting the conversation to higher ground.

. . . .
▼

Here's How it Works

▶ She just insulted me, I can't believe it! That HURTS! I am furious, scared—I feel threatened. Pause for a moment, let the comment drop . . . then try one of these responses:

"Nevertheless, we have a deadline to meet. What needs to get done here?"

"I prefer we stick to the business at hand."

"I will give what you said some thought. For now, let's focus our attention on..."

"I see you're upset. Let's explore that later. Right now we are doing. . ."

5   Shields Up

With this strategy you move back from a highly charged emotion, person, or situation and protect yourself by putting your Shields Up! Your shield may be an imagined barrier or force field that allows you to separate your emotions from others', and your reality or choices from theirs, while you think through your options.

Some people picture an imaginary shield protecting them from unproductive insults or "bubble wrap" shielding them from a screaming-toddler moment. Others roam through a highly charged event, such as a family reunion, inside a glass-topped car or "Popemobile," smiling and waving at the crowd from behind protective glass.

STRATEGIES

Here's How it Works

▶ Tammy's coworkers grow increasingly agitated about a new policy and want to pull her onto their ride. She does not have the psychic energy for this ride today, so she puts her Shield Up!, envisioning their words falling all around her, as she smiles and waves encouragement to them from behind protective glass, knowing she is not getting worked up over this one.

▶ Gregory is headed to a family reunion where he anticipates a familiar unpleasant dynamic. His mother will want to convince him what an evil man his father is--but Gregory is sick of being pulled to one side or the other. Rather than avoid the event or numb himself with alcohol, Gregory puts Shields Up! He heads to the reunion with a focus on enjoying everyone and does not allow his mom to pull him off course. When she begins her predictable tirade, Gregory imagines her words bouncing off his shields and falling harmlessly to the ground. Having chosen not to use up any emotional energy on this exchange, he is unfazed by her comments.

BUT WAIT!

 Won't my family members or coworkers sense that I am retreating from them? Will they feel I am pulling away, uncaring?

The goal here is not to "ice them out," or announce that you are removing yourself from them because they are intolerable. That might not go over too well. The goal is to protect yourself and your own vulnerable mood by adding a protective layer—a slight pause or healthy emotional distance. When you feel safe, you are actually more likely to remain positive, loving, and present. You are mastering your own emotions, picking and choosing what it is that YOU want to feel. This tactic also protects the others from your resenting them for "making you upset." You remain an adult in charge of your own mood state.

YOUR TURN

think

Think back over the past week to a situation in which you felt surprised, shocked, hurt, ignored, or had some other reaction that you do not enjoy. Describe what happened.

reflect

Now describe what you felt.

correct

Which Move Back strategy(ies) could you have used to handle it differently?

Buy Yourself Some Time
Find Your Center
Don't Go on the Ride
Let the Daggers Drop
Shields Up!

imagine

How might it have gone if you had used these strategies?

take action

Pick one strategy that you will use this week. Describe when you plan to use it.

STEP 2

observe

OBSERVE: WHAT IS IT?

Imagine that, somehow, you have been falsely led to believe that a tiger is a housecat. You step into the animal's cage and are stunned when a wild beast attacks you! This may seem like an unlikely scenario, but it conveys how astonished we can be when caught off guard by a situation we have misread—because we did not Observe it accurately. We assumed that someone was a genuine friend, a caring sister, a present parent, a nurturing supervisor, when the actual evidence suggested that that particular person was repeatedly obstructionist, self-serving, insecure, or absent. Having thought we were cuddling up to a housecat, we are devastated to discover that this person is really an untamed tiger.

That is why, once you have Moved Back, it is essential to Observe a situation objectively and factually. If you are aware of what that tigerish person is really like, you can come to the encounter more prepared. Every day, we are faced with information that reveals the nature of situations and people—at least as they are in that moment, or as they impact us—but for a variety of reasons, we don't use this data to update our interpretations. We wind up shocked, upset, angry, resentful, and hurt.

The most common reason we misread people is that we want them to be different. Here are two sample scenarios.

WHAT IS IT?

• You don't want to accept that your boss is incapable of mentoring you the way you need to be mentored—this pushes your "justice button." It's unfair!

Rather than clearly Observe and acknowledge that this boss does not provide mentorship, you stay stuck in hoping, wishing expecting or even demanding that she change. This attitude prevents you from moving on to get your mentoring somewhere else.

• Your mother does not give you the love, care, or attention you need. Naturally, you feel profoundly hurt.

At some point, though, you must just accept that—rightly or wrongly—she is unable or unwilling to give you that love you need. Otherwise you fight on, and it will be a long, draining, and unproductive emotional battle that prevents you from seeking "mothering" or nurturing from someone else who could more easily or naturally provide it.

Rather than fighting the facts, we can learn to Observe them and accept the reality they represent. Acceptance frees us to create another plan for ourselves that does allow us to get our needs met.

Here are some other common misreadings that set us up to be hurt, overwhelmed, angry, and pulled off focus:

• If we underestimate how long a project will take, we will be swamped and tanked by it—then often wind up angry at ourselves or others for misrepresenting the time required.

• If we misread our coworkers as capable, but find they lack the ability to deliver in key areas, we feel let down.

• If we overestimate our children's ability to function without our support or additional attention, they may stumble and we'll be shocked.

In this step, you learn to detach from difficult situations and objectively Observe who you are, and who the other person is, in this moment. This De-Linking, as I call it (see page 42), enables you to come up with an alternate more realistic and useful explanation of what was going on. Now you are ready to develop a more fruitful course of action.

Here Are Some More Sample Observe Scenarios:

✓ Your son does not do well in science. His repeated failure frustrates and angers you. You chose all the right schools for him; you set him up with the right books and supplies; you emphasize the importance of school—and yet this! How can it be?!

You Move Back, Pause, buy yourself some time, and Observe—without judgment, just candor. You observe that your son's poor science performance is a pattern. (Even if, in your opinion, it shouldn't be!) You need to be able to see this and accept it, rather than fight these facts or keep hoping they will change.

Observing the facts clearly—as they are, not as you hope they are—enables you to take action. You can hire a tutor. You can arrange for him to study longer hours in this subject. You can ask his teacher for suggestions. And so on. What you stop doing is remaining mad, hurt, worried, or upset. You stop staying stuck. You move from being frustrated and angry to taking action.

✓ Your colleague does not get her work done on time. As a result, your team's reports are often late and shoddy. Worrying about how this will affect your performance, you are resentful and angry. If she doesn't improve, the whole team could suffer!

You need to find a way to Move Back, Pause, and Observe. Even though she should get the work done on time, it is a fact that she does not—a fact that causes consequences which you are not in a position to change. Rather than fight this reality, it is time to see it clearly and manage around it.

Setting emotions aside, you begin to plan. How can your team as a whole get the project done on time? You move from being worried and vulnerable to being protected.

✓ Your spouse, left to his own instincts, is not likely to let you finish your sentences when you tell him something. This infuriates you! Why is he so rude?

You need to figure out how to Move Back, Pause, and buy some time. Then you can Observe that he interrupts everyone, not just you.

You don't like being interrupted, so you move to action. You find ways to teach him not to interrupt you. You move from being stuck to being creative.

BUT WAIT!

 Am I supposed to just tolerate parents, siblings, spouses, children, or bosses who fail me?

Hmmm. Tolerate is an interesting word. It implies we can "do something" about the problem. Tolerate as opposed to what? Change them? If we can change someone to meet our needs better, wonderful! Let's do it! (See, for example, the strategy Thank Forward and seeing people as "one year wiser" on page 64.) However, when we have tried repeatedly—asking, begging, coaching, consulting, and mirroring what we want—and this person still does not meet our needs, it is time to face the facts. Sadly, it is not up to us to alter these facts; we can only face them. The Observe strategies enable us to decide when someone is not likely to meet our needs adequately, so we can move forward in our own lives.

 Do I always need to "fix" the other person in order to fix the situation?

Of course it would be nice if we could. But as just noted, that's not always possible. In either case, your own protection and self-mastery require that your expectations be realistic. You need to make an assessment based on observable data and facts—not hopes, should-be's, or could-be's. And you need to develop a plan of action.

BUT WAIT!

 If I observe someone clearly, see that they are underperforming, then face this fact and develop a plan to get things done, doesn't this mean I am rescuing them or overperforming? Isn't this a recipe for codependence?

As you will see, I never advocate that you run around rescuing others. It is essential that you get to live a reasonable life, without forever mopping up after others. You will find out more about how to prevent that in Steps 3 and 4. First, though, you learn in Step 2 simply to read people and situations accurately, rather than keep on the "hope goggles." When you see things clearly, you can develop a more informed plan for moving on.

CANDID SELF-ASSESSMENT

In addition to observing others clearly, we need to observe ourselves the same way. A Candid Self-Assessment is a productive read on yourself. It is not a damning judgment ("I am a horrible person"), nor a naïve hope or wish ("I think I can or should be perfect!").

In a Candid Self-Assessment, you move from judging yourself to observing. You take into account that everyone is great at a few things, mediocre at many, and lousy at a few others. This is true for everyone you know—those you love, and those you do not. It's simply a fact of life, neither good nor bad. It just is. No one is great at everything, and no one is horrible at everything.

With that truth clearly in mind, it is time to take a candid lap around yourself, observing from all angles. Ask honestly and objectively:

- In what areas do I excel?

- In what areas am I mediocre?

- In what areas am I pretty lousy?

- Given your answers to these questions, what types of activities would be best for you to take on and develop further? Which should you delegate to others? And what might you let go of altogether?

CANDID SELF-ASSESSMENT

Remember that you do not have to do all things or be all things to the world. Instead you are trying to discern what you can handle, what you have prioritized as a must to handle—and also what you feel like doing.

Note too that we always need to update our Candid Self-Assessment—because we change! Be sure to ask yourself these questions periodically, answering as honestly and objectively as you can:

- What do I have energy for now in my life?
- What am I no longer interested in?
- What are my highest priorities now?
- What is it time to leave behind?
- What do I need more of these days? Less of?

Without such candid self-observation, we may fall into traps like these:

▶ "I should be someone who works really late and gets the project done no matter what, so why am I so lazy?"

▶ "I should be the kind of father who takes his sons to the baseball field, so what's wrong with me that I don't want to?"

By contrast, Candid Self-Assessment sounds like this:

✓ "I wish I had the energy to work late on this project, but I simply don't. I need to let the client know it will be ready next week."

✓ "I see that some fathers like playing baseball with their sons, but, to be honest, I don't. I'll take my boys to the movies instead."

When we can assess ourselves honestly and accept who we really are, we stop acting out of guilt or resentment, or trying to be who we think others want us to be. When we are honest with ourselves about what we need, we are more able to actually obtain it.

OBSERVING WITH THE THIRD EYE

How do you develop the ability to Observe difficult situations and people candidly and clearly? A good tactic is to imagine that you are looking at the situation with a "Third Eye" or an "eye in the sky." The idea is to temporarily remove yourself from the intense emotions of an encounter and observe it from a healthy emotional distance. From this mile-high perspective, you can ask important questions:

- What's really going on here?

- How would an objective observer describe what is happening—how I am acting or being treated?

- How would that person describe how the other people here are acting and being treated?

- Is this situation urgent? Not urgent? Is it necessary?

- Is it ideal? What would a more ideal interaction look like?

People who master Third Eye observation are able to quickly and objectively move back from a situation once it becomes tense in order to reframe it and, ultimately, re-choreograph it. Anyone who wants more control over their life needs this ability! Those who can't Move Back and Observe feel continuously sucked into other people's chaos, shocked, caught off guard, pinballed around, or ruled by others. You can use the third eye to observe while applying any of the strategies that follow.

TIP

In every difficult interchange, each of us has our own unique emotional response. Take note of yours! Use whatever it is you feel when someone does or says something you don't like as both a cue that you are having this response and as a challenge to overcome. Someone else's rude or insensitive behavior may be a trigger for you, but your reaction, your feeling, is your response. You own it, and it is yours to change. Whatever that response is, note it, own it, and know that it is a dynamic you need to work on.

1 Just the Facts

Once we have moved back, we use our Third Eye to open a calm space for this critical, basic strategy: observing Just the Facts. For a moment, we drop all our hopes, wishes, fears, and interpretations. We move from thinking about what ought to be to seeing exactly what is. We move from our emotional reaction center to our logic center, in order to take a good clear look at just what is actually happening.

Here's How it Works

▶ Your boss does not show up for your regular supervisory meeting. You feel angry, mistreated, and disrespected. So you Move Back. Buy a moment. Drop the emotions, find your calm, and look at the facts.

- Does she really disrespect you? Or is she unable to manage her time properly?

- Is she being dismissive? Or is she not aware that you need to meet with her?

- Does she write you off as not worth her time? Or does she routinely fail to make time for others?

- Is she intentionally trying to harm you? Or is it just that her standard behavior pattern results in your needs being unmet?

Having observed the data objectively, you see the whole situation more clearly. You stop feeling offended and start to calm down. Now you can begin thinking about how to take action that will get you what you need.

▶ You arrive at a party where everyone else is talking and laughing together. No one notices your arrival, asks you how you are, or invites you to join them. You feel left out, snubbed, embarrassed, unimportant. You don't like this feeling at all.

So you Move Back. Buy a moment. Drop the emotions, find your calm, and look at the facts.

- Do they know you have arrived? Did you tell anyone when you planned to show up? Does anyone expect you?

- Are they in mid-conversation? Is it a good time for anyone to be looking around for a new arrival?

- Are they deliberately trying to snub you? Or is it more likely that they don't notice you because you do not engage in "notice-me" behaviors? For example, have you sauntered up to the group, asserted your way tactfully into the conversation, and said, "Hello everyone! What's going on?"

You settle in. You remind yourself, "People like me once they know me. I will give everyone a chance to get to know me. And I will find a way to insert myself into their conversation."

2 Categorize It

An ancient Chinese proverb states, "The beginning of wisdom is calling things by their right name." Categorize It, like Just the Facts, calls for scientific thinking. Once we have an accurate read on something—or, most important, on how it impacts us—we can organize it to better understand it. Much as botanists label and categorize mushrooms as "toxic" or "edible," it is useful to Categorize other people and situations in our lives in a way that makes us aware of their effect on us. We do this not to blame or judge, but to understand a situation and prepare ourselves to effectively defend against it or strategize around it.

Categorize It equips us to handle an interaction effectively, instead of walking into it blindly or naively. Think of it not as judging, but as discerning whether someone is a housecat or a tiger. Remember that we do not have to share our categorizations with others, or get people to agree with them. Other people may find our difficult person a housecat! What matters most is knowing how others impact us. This allows us to deal with people and situations more successfully.

Here's How it Works

▶ Your father hurts you again and again by insulting your basketball skills. You Move Back, Observe, and Categorize his behavior as rude and insulting. Having this category clearly in mind enables you to drop your illusions about him and come up with some tactics for responding. Now when he starts to crack those jokes about how badly you play, you'll be able to protect yourself better. Exactly how you respond will depend on your own personality and your father's ability to hear what you say. You can keep several ideas in your back pocket. For example:

> Redirect or distract: "What's on TV?"

> Blow it off to yourself: "I saw that one coming!"

> Ask him directly not to criticize: "Dad, I prefer you just high-five me after the games."

> Use humor or sarcasm: "Hmm, I didn't realize you've been inducted into the basketball hall of fame, Dad."

▶ You notice that Timothy berates others to make himself look good. You Categorize him as insecure. Realizing this, you do not feel insulted, put down, or embarrassed by his public comments about you, but simply consider your choices for responding. Possibilities:

> Redirect: "Say, what did you hear about the Johnson project?"

> Use sarcasm: "Timothy, with those kinds of comments you'll be President-elect in no time!"

> Deflect, in your head: "Small-minded human behavior. Somebody clearly didn't get a hug this morning before he left home."

▶ Your workplace atmosphere is unprofessional. People gossip too much and do not focus on their work. It pulls you off focus. You want to be productive in order to get a good review when you change jobs. You realize that you need to stay out of the gossiping. Some choices:

> Deflect: Nod and say "You said it," as you turn your attention back to your project.

> Remove yourself: Take a path from your desk to the break room that does not send you directly through the gossip swirl.

> Shield yourself: Take a book and appear engrossed when others start a conversation that you prefer not to engage.

BUT WAIT!

 Why should I have to change? The other person is the problem!

Observe clearly. You have a problem with this person. It is your problem. Every day, same problem. It is yours to solve. The other does not have a problem with his behavior—you do. You solve it so that YOU don't have it any longer.

3 | De-Link

De-Linking is powerful. It enables us to see ourselves as apart—de-linked—from painful or upsetting people and events. It allows us to separate our integrity, reputation, or emotions from challenging, hurtful, or unprofessional people and situations. It even allows us to separate our current selves from a prior, less evolved version of us.

Too often we over-identify with others. We see them as a reflection of us, when in fact, what most defines who we are today is our own current actions. Yet we might still feel identified with an alcoholic parent or misbehaving child and expect that we should or will be judged by that other person's behavior. We may believe that an underperforming company we work for—or own—will follow us through life and ruin our reputation forever. We may feel the weight of a painful relationship that ended in divorce, fearing it reflects who we are and ever will be. We may worry that a disappointing interaction with our adult children reflects how they will always perceive us.

We De-Link by consciously acknowledging that we are not forever connected with other people, our distant past, or even the mistake we made yesterday. Once we realize this, we can start fresh by choosing what we do want to be linked with. Starting now.

The truth is that each day is a new day, bringing new opportunities to De-Link, Skill Up, and become someone slightly better—someone who can behave differently, choose a new job, or move into a new relationship. Other people's actions or abilities—or even our prior selves—do not damn us forever.

Here's How it Works

▶ My father is an alcoholic. This concerns me greatly because when he drinks, he is not there for me, and he makes poor choices. I do not want to be like him.

> De-Link: I remind myself that I am not him: I can make other choices. I De-Link myself from his choices. I remain more vigilant about how much I drink and how I honor my commitments to my family. I surround myself with people who can be there for me in ways he cannot.

▶ I underperformed in my old job. This worries me! What if I am always going to be an underperformer? What if the world comes to know me as a bad or weak worker?

> De-Link: I know I am separate now from that experience. I choose to learn new skills to become more professional.

▶ My boss does not know how to mentor. I am frustrated, and also worried. What if I don't learn the tools and processes of this job? How will I ever learn or develop? Will I be exposed as not knowing what I should? I have asked for mentoring, meetings, on-ramping, development, but he never provides it!

> De-Link: Having observed this situation clearly, I see that I need to De-Link myself from being mentored by this boss. I choose to get good mentoring from an outside source, even if I have to pay for it myself.

▶ My company is failing. I am scared. What if people assume that I am bad, too? I do not want my lifelong reputation to be tied to this failing business that I started.

> De-Link: I De-Link myself from this failed effort and will work to find a new job, a new career path, and a new source of income. I choose to start carving an identity for myself as someone who can see when it is time to begin a venture, and also when to end it. I think of myself as someone who had the good judgment to close the business at the right time.

TIP

If you do not De-Link, you might stay attached to a failing business or relationship for too long! De-linking and moving on allow you to be more successful in the long run.

4 | Put on the Translator

One reason we misinterpret situations and interactions is that we misunderstand other people's intentions and behaviors. We need to keep in mind that we interpret any comments, actions, and events through our personal lens. And that lens is often clouded by our own issues, insecurities, or needs. This strategy enables you to slow down and consider before you attach interpretations to a situation that carry all kinds of unpleasant baggage.

When we Put on the Translator, we give ourselves an alternate interpretation of something that upsets us. When someone triggers an emotional reaction, after moving back and pausing, ask yourself, "What interpretation have I made that is painful here?"

Then take a disciplined moment to translate the other person's behavior more objectively. Look for other ways of viewing the situation—other translations. Don't leap at the first interpretation that comes to you. Instead, Observe the facts. Ask yourself, "What do I feel? How did I translate that?" Then ask yourself whether there are other possible translations.

> Here's How it Works

▶ Your husband demands: Why did you set that there?

> Your first reaction: He doesn't like how I do things. He is questioning me. He doesn't love me.

> Observation: This translation is painful. It feels like he'll never love me. But is it an accurate interpretation? I will drop it and look at the facts.

> Facts: He's not very organized himself and really needs to know where things are. Is there a translation that allows me to stay more neutral or even loving?

> Translation: He is really just asking where it usually goes, and how he will find it next time if I don't put it there today. He's yelling at me because he's frazzled.

▶ Your four-year-old screams: I hate this school! Everyone is mean, and I want to stay home!

> Your first reaction: Oh no! Allie is anxious and weak. What if I am raising a timid girl?

> Observation: I see that I am blaming myself and reacting out of fear. And it is clear that my being worked up is getting Allie more worked up and reinforcing the pattern. What are the facts here?

> Facts: How often has she reacted this way? Is it true that she has no friends? Actually the other day she came home and told me she had a fine day. Perhaps this state of hers isn't permanent.

> Translation: Allie is having a bad day. She doesn't yet have the skills to handle new kids and new situations. She needs help figuring it all out.

▶ Your teenager exclaims: Why don't you ever let me do what I need to do? You smother me! Other kids get to go out all the time!

> Your first reaction: Jimmy is clueless and disrespectful. He is attacking my parenting style.

> Observation: Lashing out at him for saying this and demanding he respect me gets me nowhere. This argument goes on and on. I get all worked up when he says this, and that doesn't help. What is really going on here?

> Facts: I am not the kind of parent who keeps my son under lock and key. I let Jimmy go to parties and events, but this particular party is one I do not wish him to attend. There will be no parents home at that house. I need to find a way to broach this conversation with Jimmy.

> Translation: Jimmy is wondering how he can explain why he isn't at the party. He's not sure if he even wants to go, but he doesn't want to say he's not there because his parents made him stay home. Jimmy needs help managing peer pressure in ways that keep his identity intact.

> **BUT WAIT!**

 What if my first reaction was right? That person really IS threatening me, or is anxious, or does disrespect me?

Sometimes we are right the first time. After moving back from highly charged emotions, observing candidly, and thinking through several possible interpretations, we may conclude that our initial assessment is correct and needs no translation. But since we have paused, our response is likely to be less charged, calmer, and more productive in handling that reality.

5 Check the Guilt

Guilt is both ubiquitous and wildly unproductive. Guilt is useful when—and only when—we use it as a cue to take action or change something in our lives. If we have no intention or need to change, guilt only serves to keep us from fully accepting ourselves.

Guilt prevents us from paying attention to what we want for our life. When we operate out of guilt, we are often unknowingly trying to fulfill others' goals for us (or our perceptions of those goals), rather than pursuing our own highest goals and authoring our life ourselves.

The trick is to observe these dynamics, do some Candid Self-Assessment, and Check the Guilt. There is no reason to cling to it. If we realize it is not related to OUR highest goal, we need to "check it at the door." It may belong to someone else, which makes it theirs. Not ours.

Guilt that is telling us something we really need to hear (such as: "I need to be a calmer parent" or "I need to pay more attention at work") does belong to us. In that case, we need to take it as a call to action and make a change!

But if your guilt is actually a reaction to someone else's wish for you, it is time to grow up and check it. You do this by observing, "Whose guilt is this? Whose message does it convey? Is it mine? Then I'll make a change. If it does not apply to me, I will drop it or hand it back to the one it belongs to."

> ### Here's How it Works

▶ I feel guilty saying no to the community project. I don't want to let people down. But I don't like working on it, I don't grow from doing it, and I don't want to continue doing it year after year.

> Check the Guilt: Is this my goal—to keep volunteering? Or is it someone else's goal that I keep carrying this load? Am I doing this because I want to and it fulfills me, or to please others so I can hear them say, "You're great!" I observe that this is their goal for me, no longer my goal for me. I have outgrown it.
>
> You say: In the past, I have helped on the project a great deal. But this year I have other priorities I must attend to. Thank you for understanding.

▶ I feel guilty for loving Sarah. My parents think less of me for it. Yet I don't think less of me for loving her, and I don't intend to stop loving her

> Check the Guilt: Do I really feel guilty for loving her, or for not loving the person they want me to love? Whose problem is this? I observe that I like loving Sarah just fine.

> You say: Sarah may not appear to be the type of person you would have chosen for me. Yet with time, I hope you will come to see what I see in her—someone who makes my life better.

▶ I feel guilty for not doing more at work. The other guys stay late, attend dinners with the boss, and go that extra yard. But that's not who I want to be, or how I want to live. I don't intend to work eighty hours a week; I intend to do my job well and clock out on time, so I have a good quality of home life.

> Check the Guilt: Who wants me to be a workaholic? Not me. They might have a problem with my going home, but I really value being a present father to my children and husband to my spouse.

> You say: Enjoy the dinner, guys. I've got a family that wants me home. See you in the office tomorrow at nine.

6 Doable versus Advisable

For all the heroes and superheroes out there, anything is Doable! But at a price. It is important to ask: what are the costs of taking something on—to your time, your sleep, your sanity, your leisure, happiness, health, or other life goals?

Instead of asking, "Can I do it?" try candidly assessing yourself, asking, "At what cost?" Move back from the emotions, ego temptations, or guilt provocations of the situation, observe candidly, and ask, "Is it Advisable?" More specifically, ask: "At this time, at this level, with these people, under these conditions, in this way, is it advisable for me to get involved?"

> Here's How it Works

▶ Someone at a meeting says: "Would you chair this committee? You'd be perfect!"

You ask:

> Is it Doable? I am overworked as it is, and I promised to exercise more and spend time with friends. I do not feel good about taking on this committee. But . . . it is doable, I suppose, if I wake up earlier each day . . .

> Is it Advisable? Sure, I can do it. I can do just about anything I set my mind to. However, given my goals of self-care, improved health, and connecting with friends, it is not advisable at this time.

You say: I appreciate your thinking of me. Another time, perhaps. This year, I have other commitments I must attend to.

▶ Your child pleads: "Mommy, can we go to the park today? Can we, can we? It's sunny and warm and I don't have any homework tonight!"

You ask:

> Is it Doable? Yes, and it would make her happy. I have a big engagement tomorrow and I was really counting on cleaning the house tonight, but I suppose I could stay up all night cleaning and get it done.

> Is it Advisable? If I went to the park today, I would pay a high price. I've committed to living a more balanced life. I am tired of working to the bone just to make others happy, only to find I let them down the next day by being cranky or resentful! I need to find a way to balance my needs and hers.

You Say: Not today, pumpkin. We've got cleaning to do! Let's put it on the calendar for Saturday.

YOUR TURN

think

Think back over the past week to a situation in which you felt surprised, shocked, hurt, ignored, or had some other reaction that you do not enjoy. Describe what happened.

reflect

Now describe what you felt.

correct

Which Observe strategy(ies) could you have used to handle it differently?

Just the Facts
Categorize It
De-Link
Put on the Translator
Guilt Check
Doable versus Advisable

imagine

How might it have gone if you had used these strategies?

take action

Pick one strategy that you will use this week. Describe when you plan to use it.

STEP 3

visualize

VISUALIZE: WHAT IS IT?

Once we have moved back and observed, it is time to visualize. Visualize requires replacing our familiar negative landscape with an optimistic one that is more productive, fulfilling, and rewarding. It requires imagining a new landscape for a problematic relationship or situation. What is important is to begin moving forward, going somewhere we have never gone before.

> **BUT WAIT!**

 How can I do this if things are really bad or scary in my life? Don't I need to stay where I am and deal with these things?

Visualize uses the skill of Looking Ahead—to somewhere healthier (see page 49). This is hard to do, often because when we are in our most stuck places, we cannot clearly see what "better" looks like!

The fact is that moving forward in life means going somewhere we have never been. I am asking that after you Move Back and Observe, you Visualize a new place for yourself in relation to that difficult person or situation—then use the new skills of this step to begin intentionally choreographing that scene. These are the strategies of visualizing.

A helpful age-old analogy here is driving a car. When we drive, we need to glance at the rear-view mirror occasionally to see the things we have passed. But when we drive forward, how much time should we spend looking in the rear-view mirror? Eighty percent? Sixty? More like ten percent, given that we are operating a moving vehicle. Otherwise we will either crash or never find our destination.

To reach this destination where we have not yet been, we must spend most of our time looking out the front windshield. And we often also need a map to guide us—a type of visualization.

WHAT IS IT?

Moving forward in life, past old dynamics and real obstacles, requires us to visualize distinctly and realistically where we want to go. Many people are very clear about what they don't want for their life. They come to my office saying, "I hate my boss; I'm angry at my spouse; I'm tired of being rejected; I'm sad and lonely." It's good to know what we don't want; that's a start. But moving forward requires us to clearly identify what we DO want.

Do you know what you want? What exactly does that look like? The more clearly and specifically we Visualize what we want, the more effectively we can set to work making it happen.

Here Are Some Sample Visualize Scenarios:

✓ Marietta's ten-year-old daughter, Chelsie, is rude. She interrupts, talks over others, makes plans and cancels them on a dime, and seems not to care about her friends' feelings or choices. This triggers Marietta, whose father was narcissistic—he talked incessantly about his career and rarely focused his attention on Marietta. Each time she sees Chelsie being rude, Marietta reacts, fearing that her daughter will become narcissistic.

Marietta Moves Back, Observes the facts and her interpretations, and decides she needs to De-Link her feelings about her relationship with her father from her feelings about her relationship with her daughter.

Working to Visualize a better outcome for Chelsie, she begins to see a view out the front windshield that is more positive. Instead of picturing Chelsie growing into a self-centered woman, she opts to imagine Chelsie maturing into a friendly person. She visualizes Chelsie becoming more friendly, more attentive, and more considerate toward others each day.

Rather than chase after Chelsie with comments like, "Don't be so rude!" or "Why are you so mean to your friends?" (comments that could unintentionally mold a negative self-identity in a child), Marietta makes empowering suggestions like, "Chelsie, be a love and see what your friends would like to drink" or "Chelsie, as gracious hosts, shall we go see what your friends would like to do now?"

Rather than get stuck asking, "Why should I need to teach my daughter this?" Marietta remains determined to teach Chelsie all she can about noticing and appreciating others. Before long Marietta sees a change in Chelsie's behavior from oblivious to attentive, and her own mood shifts from fearful to relieved.

✓ Brendan was let go from his job of ten years. He is understandably afraid about his future. What if he can't find another job? What if he won't be able to pay his mortgage? As his fears take root, he becomes much more self-doubting than he ever was, pessimistic, bitter. He knows this can only harm him in interviews and interactions with people in his network. He needs to find ways to move forward.

After Moving Back and taking time to Observe and express his feelings and thoughts, Brendan chooses to Visualize a positive future that he has never seen before. He gives himself permission to ask, "What if something good happens to me that I never imagined possible?" "What if I can see myself making new things happen for myself?" "What if I believe I am worthy, competent, and resilient, and I know that others will see me this way, too?"

Brendan sets to work picturing positive options opening to him. He persists in meeting with colleagues for lunches and interviews. He resists succumbing to depression, challenging himself to keep his eyes on the front windshield and away from the rear-view mirror. In time, he is happy to receive a couple of promising offers.

BUT WAIT!

Maybe Brendan is just super-skilled and would have gotten a job anyway! Visualization wasn't what got him the job, his skills did!

Perhaps, but even so, why waste time feeling so negative in the meantime? Or worse, developing symptoms of real stress, anxiety, or depression that impair our physical health, sleep patterns, emotional well-being, and relationships?

What about someone who doesn't have Brendan's skills and doesn't get a job? Wouldn't positive visualization just set them up for a huge disappointment? That would be a bitter pill to swallow.

Hmmm, sounds like someone is thinking pretty negatively. Something is possible for everyone. Visualization is not about creating a myth or a fantasy. It is about seeing something exciting that is realistic and could happen. It involves seeing your strengths and opportunities more clearly than your deficits and liabilities. It combines a positive self-view with imagining actual pathways that could lead to things opening up for you. Most of all, it is about stopping the habit of closing off doors to your future instead of knocking on them.

Watch out for the tendency to hold back due to fear of hard times. Hard times are just hard times. They do not kill us, they only challenge us. If we know how to get back on our feet—and believe that we can and will—we can stay in the game, no matter what it takes.

STRATEGIES

1 | Look Ahead

We set the stage for getting where we want to be by Looking Ahead. This strategy asks us to look forward and define clearly what it is we want more of. We often have a distinct vision of what we want less of (a screaming spouse, a mean neighbor, a dead-end job). But can we Look Ahead and see something different? As the saying goes, "If you don't know where you are headed, how will you get there?" This is true for all the paths we follow in life. When we look ahead, we force ourselves to "go shopping" by looking around for something better. What is "better"? Who has it? What does it look like? And how can I get some? Spend as much time as you can shopping for "better."

- What does "good" look like on other people? What would a better relationship, job, family life, sense of self look or feel like?
- Who has something that looks like it would feel better for you?
- What did they do to get to the point where they could have it?
- How might that be possible for you?
- How would it look in your world?

TIP

Often we do not actually know anyone who embodies what we want more of in our lives—this is why we are stuck! In that case, it's great to begin with a celebrity, or even a fictional character, who we imagine has these qualities. Then we borrow from that person. Examples my clients have used:

- Claire Huxtable, the wife on "The Cosby Show," was one client's archetype of a confident yet loving, assertive yet giving woman who made her way in the world without becoming bitter or vicious.

- Another client chose Audrey Hepburn as the image of a generous woman who could promote her own career while championing the causes of others.

- For a third client, Sean Connery was the archetype for a man who remains calm under pressure.

Then you can ask, "What would ___ do?" filling in your archetype's name. You imagine what that person would do in various challenge scenarios, and apply the strength, ideas, behaviors, and even words you come up with to your own tough spots. Looking ahead—even if only in your imagination!—is far more productive than spinning in an unhappy past.

Here's How it Works

▶ You are exhausted all the time. You work late hours, come home, cook and clean, stay up working some more, get up early, and do it all again the next day. You know you are working too much. You know you don't like it. It is time to Visualize what you DO want.

Look Ahead: What do you want more of? You answer: peace, relaxation, downtime.

Visualize: You set to work visualizing what peaceful relaxation actually looks like. You imagine what activities a peaceful person might engage in:

- Put his feet up for twenty minutes after arriving home from work;

- Take twenty minutes of quiet time to listen to peaceful music before the kids rush home;

- Light a candle to create a calming mood before dinner;

- Take a minute to repeat a calm message to herself: "Good job getting through the day," "You have done all you need to do for today," or "You can let it go now."

Then, just as important, you spend time picturing what a peaceful person chooses not to do:

- Rush from meeting to meeting;
- Schedule three meetings in one day;
- Make calls on the way to work;
- Squeeze in "one more thing" by stopping at the store on the way out of town.

Now you make a commitment to yourself that tomorrow, you will do one thing on the peaceful "do" list and remove one thing from the "do not do" list.

Go Shopping: Who around you looks peaceful and relaxed? Is there someone you know and respect who creates and maintains downtime in their life? You realize you only know two types of people: overworked folks like yourself and slackers. Clearly you need to "go shopping" for relaxed people who also work well.

After a week of shopping around for people who enjoy downtime, you come up with a woman in your apartment building, an executive manager who finds time to garden. Contemplating her example, you begin to see how you too might be able to create downtime for yourself.

▶ You regret how much you yell every morning as you race to get out the door. "Where are my keys? Where is my coat!" You are tired of being irritated and rushed.

> Look Ahead: What do you want more of? Answer: being calm and on time. What would that feel like?

> Go Shopping: Who do you know who is on time and calm? You picture your grandmother, who always takes her time, whatever she is doing. Rather than reject this example because she is retired and no longer has to hurry to work, you take it in for a minute. You imagine: "What if I had more time—all the time in the world—and did not have to live life feeling so rushed?"

> Visualize: You begin to Visualize a calm, organized morning. What would you need to do to move through every morning calm, on time, and in control? You use your visualization to plan out your week accordingly, making a place for your keys and coat, waking up ten minutes earlier, and committing to this new vision of yourself.

2 180 Degrees

The 180 Degrees strategy takes visualization a step further by going into more detail. It asks you to clearly define the 180-degree opposite of whatever it is you dislike and want to change. This exercise forces you to put into words or to Visualize the exact change you do want. Naming it to yourself clearly and specifically shifts your energy away from your previous focus on what you don't want. It forces you to name what you do want and begin focusing your time and energy on getting it—rather than being angry, hurt, or upset about what you dislike.

Knowing what we DO want, naming it, and visualizing it enables us to begin to go after it. If we do not visualize what we want, we are not likely to go to work getting it.

- Instead of spending time ruminating over how rude and disrespectful your daughter is, visualize what you do want from her: respect, consideration.

- Instead of feeling that everyone at work thinks you're a pushover and takes advantage of you by handing you extra work, start visualizing how you want them to think of you and treat you: with respect, as someone to be taken seriously—someone whom they ask before handing work to.

Here's How it Works

▶ You are tired of having the same argument with your teenager. It's a repeating pattern in which you ask her a question about school and she blows up at you. For example, when you ask, "How did chemistry go today?" she shoots back, "Why does everything have to matter so much to you? Why do you meddle? Why can't you just live your own life and not pry into mine?!"

What you want to stop: Feeling put down, belittled, being hollered at by her.

Its 180-Degree Opposite: I want to communicate calmly and effectively with my daughter. I want her to find ways to talk with me respectfully, I want her to know I support and love her, and I want her to be kind in her interaction with me, as I will be with her.

Put the opposite into action: When she begins to yell, you pause and say gently, "What I am asking is how you are. You matter to me. If you want to change the subject, please do so."

▶ You dislike being overlooked at work. Other people steal your ideas and get credit—are even promoted—while you spend precious years at the lower end of the ladder.

What you want to stop: Being overlooked, being brushed off.

Its 180-Degree Opposite: I want to be taken seriously at work. I want people to notice that I have ideas, abilities, and worth. I want recognition.

Put the opposite into action: I see that I need to go to work to get that recognition. I will find ways to feel appreciated for what I do and to be considered on important matters. I will ask colleagues to run ideas past me; to consult me before sending work out of the office; to align with me before moving a project up the chain. I will routinely keep my boss apprised of my key achievements.

TIP

In both these scenarios, you do not wait for the other person to change 180 Degrees; you visualize and choreograph a 180-degree change in yourself.

VISUALIZE V 👁

3 Labyrinth

The Labyrinth is a powerful image for life. It comes from Alice Eagly and Linda Carli's book Through the Labyrinth: The Truth About How Women Become Leaders. Eagly and Carli chronicle how certain women succeed in rising to the top in their careers despite real, tangible barriers. They do this not through luck or privilege (although both help). These women succeed by remaining resilient and vigilant in looking for alternate paths when seemingly impassable roadblocks appear.

I love this image. I encourage clients to think of life as a Labyrinth by telling them:

- When you hit a wall that feels real, insurmountable, and unfair: stop, dust yourself off, and consider . . . is there another way?

Here's How it Works

▶ Linda feels that her marriage stifles her and holds her back from having a career or any personal interests that consume significant amounts of time. She has not been able to talk to her husband about these feelings, but now that her kids are grown and out of the house, she is ready to find a way to devote more of her time to goals of her own.

Through the Labyrinth: Having observed her feelings, Linda decides she needs some help. She seeks out a career counselor to help her re-enter the workforce. She has a candid conversation with her husband about this decision. During this discussion she finds that her husband may not be as supportive as she'd like, but will not stand in her way.

▶ Donald needs his partner to sign a business agreement so that their company can move in a new direction. The partner is dragging his feet. For Donald, this stalling and objecting is like a brick wall that he can't get past.

Through the Labyrinth: Donald explores other strategies for creating the deal and for influencing his partner. He believes that if he stays creative, optimistic, and on the alert for open windows, something will move forward—somehow, some way. At length Donald figures out how to restructure the agreement so that it will be implemented over a longer period of time and with different terms, which his partner finds more agreeable.

4 Thrive Alongside

Moving forward requires us to see life as a win-win proposition. It is not acceptable to be the "loser" in every relationship or situation. Watch out for the tendency toward self-sacrifice and martyrdom that keeps so many people from achieving contentment and life-realization. Moving forward means that we consider our own needs, too.

It is not necessary to ignore others in order to get ahead ourselves. We simply need to Thrive Alongside and make our needs count, too.

Here's How it Works

▶ Josh is a hard-working attorney and parent of three. When he gets home from work, his wife, exhausted from the day, hands the children over and announces, "I need some me time."

Josh is tempted to object: "Hold on! I just got home from working all day! At least YOU could take a break if you wanted to!" But he knows these comments sting her, make her cry, make her feel trapped and worthless—or worse, unleash an attack back at him: "You think YOU work all day?! Try cooking, cleaning, wiping faces, cleaning up vomit, taking out the trash . . . You don't know what hard work is! You sit at a desk all day!"

So Josh is determined to avoid a fight over who works hardest. They both work hard, and they need to be a team. At the same time, Josh is unwilling to "cave" and take care of his wife's needs but not his own.

Thrive Alongside : Josh comes up with a creative way to give his wife a much-needed break and get some recuperation time himself between the rat race and the "second shift." He responds, "Boy, I really understand. My day's been crazy and I could use some of that, too. How about if I take the kids outside and run off some energy with them while you take an hour for yourself? Maybe we have something simple like pasta for dinner? And then I'd like to watch the ball game after dinner while you put them to bed. Does that sound OK?"

▶ Ann has two adult children, both with kids of their own. She wants to be an available grandmother, but she also is ready for "her turn." So she's begun taking classes at a local university. Her son calls to ask if he can drop off the kids this weekend so he can attend a wedding.

Move Back and Observe: Ann Pauses, Moves Back, and Observes the situation. She'd like to help out; she knows her son and his wife need their time together without the kids. At the same time, she needs time for herself.

Thrive Alongside: "Wow, a wedding sounds like fun, and I know you and Lisa need some time alone. I would love to help. I have my class until three. Tell you what. Find coverage until three, then I can step in and take over from there."

TIP

Your cue here is resentment. Imagine that you have been given a "Resent-O-Meter." Be aware of the moment that the needle crosses the line from "giving happily" or "giving in important ways I feel proud of" to "feeling resentful." This is your cue that it is time to listen to your own needs. You very well may need to focus on the other person less and start thriving for yourself a little more.

Does this strategy strike you as selfish? Interesting response. I notice that when we give past our resentment line, we begin having very negative feelings—anger and even hate—toward other people, even those we love. In fact, it is far more loving to give from a place of wholeness that does not deny your own humanity, limitations, and needs.

Remember too that when you feel resentful, it is because of something you are doing to yourself. You are allowing someone to steal too much of your time. You are allowing someone to drain your afternoon. You are allowing them to interrupt you or push you past your comfort point of giving. They can ask, but only you can over-give. The moment you cross that resentment line, it is time to pause, step back, and think of a way to dial up your own needs a little more.

5 Coach Forward/Thank Forward

This strategy implies that you see both other people and yourself as always growing. Drawing from a vision of people as continually improving, Coach Forward sees them as "one year wiser."

In this strategy, rather than feeling stuck, trapped, or hopeless and assuming things will never change, you Visualize another person or scenario as "one year better" and begin to choreograph that change by "coaching it forward," offering the person suggestions for what you want to see happen, rather than digging in critically about what she or he is currently doing that you do not like.

We can also Thank Forward. When someone's objectionable behavior or failure to help sets off our Resent-O-Meter, we can pause and imagine the 180-Degree opposite: what we would prefer were happening. Then we thank the other in advance for helping us make it happen.

When you put Coach/Thank Forward into practice, you will soon find out what you can expect from someone. (Some people won't change, but let's try this strategy on those we sure hope will!)

You will be astonished at how effective Coach Forward is. It is a very powerful tool because it leaves little to chance or to just hoping that "things will work out better next time." Instead, you specifically picture what you would like others to say and do differently, and you adopt a posture as helper/assistant/coach/tutor (rather than exasperated, resentful victim). In this role you let them know clearly what a good outcome, response, or behavior looks and sounds like.

Here's How it Works

▶ Your coworker Leanne uses rude, abrupt language in the office to complain about clients. This concerns you. You do not want visiting clients to overhear this kind of talk and think that you are an unprofessional group of people.

> Coach Forward: Instead of assuming Leanne will always be rude, you decide to Visualize her having a more polished, polite manner. You coach her forward by interrupting her like this:
>
> "Hold up, Leanne. We are all professionals here and you yourself excel at project plans. I'll bet you can find a way to manage that client situation tactfully and proactively in ways that make us all look good."

▶ You are hurt that your girlfriend dotes on her friends and family members but spends little time lately asking about your day. You begin to feel taken for granted and to worry that she might be overlooking you, assuming you don't need her time and attention, when, in truth, you do.

> Coach Forward: You Visualize her being more attentive and affectionate. Rather than dive into a whiny lecture and demand, "Why do you love other people more than me?" you coach her forward in a loving, clear, productive, and adult way:
>
> "You know what I love? When you surprise me with cards and emails asking about my day. You are such a thoughtful person, and when you do that, I feel so cared for."

▶ You are busy taking care of bills when your fifteen-year-old barges into your office insisting, "I need this form filled out right now!" You feel yourself getting worked up and resentful. You think: she is going to wreck my night!

Coach Forward: You Move Back, Observe, and Visualize. You do not want to yell. You do not want to be interrupted. You do not want to resent. You Visualize two mature people working well together to meet the needs that need meeting. So you thank her forward:

"Thank you for understanding that I am swamped at the moment. Just leave it in the kitchen where I can find it when I am able to give it my full attention."

TIP

Most of us know instinctively that complaining about what we don't like falls on deaf ears. Who wants to hear: "I don't like it when you . . ." or "Why do you have to be so . . .?" Coach Forward stops that type of negative expression. Instead it draws on positive visualization of what works and sounds better and actually helps move people into a better place:

- "Be a love and hand me . . ."
- "I love it when you ask me this way . . ."
- "Thanks in advance for getting your chores done before grandma comes."
- "It helps tremendously when you . . ."

Can you hear the better energy? That's leading with class.

BUT WAIT!

Thanking someone forward seems kind of manipulative or patronizing.

Tone and timing are important. So is knowing the other person well. You do not want to come across as rude, condescending, or controlling. As for being manipulative—think rather strategic. We manipulate (read also "influence") other people with just about everything we say.

Keep clearly in mind that when you coach or thank someone forward, you are visualizing him behaving in ways that HE will be proud of too! You are actually empowering him to be a lovelier person. Be careful not to assume that this is a transaction in which you win and the other loses. Indeed, in most of our relationships, if you win, the other wins too, and both of you move further along.

YOUR TURN

think

Think back over the past week to a situation in which you felt surprised, shocked, hurt, ignored, or had some other reaction that you do not enjoy. Describe what happened.

reflect

Now describe what you felt.

correct

Which Visualize strategy(ies) could you have used to handle it differently?

Look Ahead
180 Degrees
Labyrinth
Thrive Alongside
Coach Forward/Thank Forward

imagine

How might it have gone if you had used these strategies?

take action

Write down three things you will do differently this week to have more control over your life.

STEP 4

E

evolve

EVOLVE: WHAT IS IT?

Once you have Moved Back, Observed, and Visualized a better way of living, interacting, and feeling, it is time to Evolve so that you are no longer a person who can become easily provoked or thrown off course. An evolved version of you is rehearsed and ready for whatever comes your way. You are less shocked by others' behavior or by challenging situations; you are prepared, you are properly De-Linked—perhaps you even become Entertained? (That is a strategy—see page 81.)

Evolving means committing to being a smoother, calmer person. You take the time to learn and grow from each trigger moment of today or even yesterday. You dedicate yourself to being ready for tomorrow by doing real work now! You prepare and Rehearse (see page 75) with real discipline, using new techniques and strategies that are effective and mature. You understand that when someone else triggers you, it is less a sign that they should change (Darn! We wish!) than an invitation for you to evolve. When you accept this, you are ready to move into Step 4 and begin the work of evolving into someone who is not triggered easily or for long.

An evolved person is simply an adult, at all times. She or he is no longer triggered into acting like a powerless child but has become an adult who recognizes and uses her power and options.

Note that I am not suggesting you will ever be "trigger-free." To live among humans is to be triggered. However, an evolved you will be masterful at pausing, moving back, observing, visualizing, and moving forward. Eventually you will reach a point where the trigger evokes only a mild response and—most important—you remain an adult.

THE DRAMA TRIANGLE

The concept of the Drama Triangle is quite helpful to keep in mind as you use the Evolve strategies. Developed decades ago by psychotherapist Stephen Karpman, it describes three typical roles people assume in any human interaction: the Rescuer, the Victim, or the Adult.

> • Rescuers spend excess energy fixing other people's problems, sometimes at the expense of their own needs, and often when others don't even ask for help. They are martyrs, fixers, heroes, on the lookout to prevent bad things from happening. It is exhausting to be a Rescuer, and often unrewarding. Rescuers can be heard saying, "I was just trying to help!"

> • Victims cannot seem to win. People take advantage of them. They get the bum end of the stick. They are unable to find a way to gain and keep power, authority, or respect. They tend to feel a great deal of resentment and anger at others for having power over them or doing things to them, and to blame those others. They can be heard saying, "Why don't I ever get a fair shake? Why do I always lose? Why do people keep me from getting what I need?"

> • Adults may rescue others and become victimized temporarily, but they do not remain in either role for long. They find a way to regain their center and "return to adult." Adults know what they need and find a way to get it—somehow, some way. They do not blame others for getting in their way; they just blaze a new trail. They are optimistic, hardy, resilient. They move through the Labyrinth rather than remain stuck. They succeed.

Evolve challenges you to become and remain an adult in all your encounters, especially the most difficult ones. The strategies of Step 4 offer guidance for re-righting yourself and regaining your center. They shore you up during the work of remaining an adult.

The Evolve strategies enable us to be prepared when triggers occur. Using them is like practicing review questions before the test, so the test itself is easy. It is like training six months before a marathon so the race is more manageable. We evolve by committing ourselves to practicing good strategies each day, strategies that allow us to achieve polish, poise, and presence.

Here Are Some Sample Evolve Scenarios:

✓ Valerie, a working mother of four, is tired of having screaming matches every morning as she tries to get herself and her children out the door. Every day, anger at her children and regret for how she treats them are followed by huge surges of guilt in which she tells herself she is a lousy mom and a lousy person. These battles leave her feeling hopeless and frustrated. She is aware that promising herself that "tomorrow will be different" is a hope—not a strategy.

Move Back : Valerie sets aside some "alone time" to think through this situation.

Observe: She identifies her trigger moments by writing down on a piece of paper the specific parts of the morning that go wrong day after day: clothes not where they should be, shoes missing, kids not keeping track of their belongings, lunches not packed, keys missing, whining by the five-year-old, and schoolbooks not in backpacks. Valerie also Observes that some of these problems are hers to correct and some are her children's. She recognizes that she has been over-doing their chores in an attempt to "rescue" them from being late each morning, rather than setting an expectation ahead of time that they will be more responsible.

Visualize: Valerie Visualizes a "smooth" morning: "What would it look like if I were happy and calm, and the kids were taking on responsibilities they can handle?"

Check the Guilt: She stops beating herself up and instead asks, "How can I help myself improve this situation?"

Rehearse: Valerie begins preparing, planning, and rehearsing her morning routine, including four or five ready lines to say to the children: "Books in bags." "Kids in car." "Ready or not, here we go." "No shoes? Oh well. Socks today, and tomorrow, you'll have your shoes ready."

✓ Keith likes being on time to social events. His wife, Marybeth, resents them as an "added headache," so she tends to drag her feet. Keith is tired of arguing with Marybeth over her making him late; tired of feeling like the victim of her behavior. He decides to find a way to be an evolved adult who knows what he wants and makes it happen.

> Move Back: Before the next trigger event, Keith gives himself time to explore his pattern with Marybeth and ask a few questions.
>
> Observe: Although he wants to be on time, he has been unwilling to go alone, because he feels more secure showing up with someone. He notices that his anger at Marybeth is really about her not "rescuing" him by satisfying his need to be with someone. He also recognizes that she does not like this type of public event and should not have to attend them repeatedly if she does not want to. He sees that his need to have her with him is his problem, not hers. In fact she has been more than reasonable by going to one or two events a year.
>
> Visualize: Keith decides to Visualize himself as an adult, not a resentful child angry at his wife for not making him feel more secure. He pictures himself arriving on time, feeling secure somehow—but how?
>
> Evolve: Keith prepares for the next event. First he asks himself, "How can I make that vision happen in a way that does not hinder my relationship with my wife, burden her, or set me up to be late and upset?" He sends out emails to find out who from his office might be going and asks for a ride. By connecting with other people who enjoy public events and arrive on time, he gets what he needs without putting Marybeth in the position of having power over him that neither of them wants her to have. His problem; his solution.

Evolve is not an easy step. It asks us to make very mature, and at times, very difficult decisions in order to get our needs met. And as you will see, the strategies require tough actions, often involving giving up or letting go. Evolving challenges us: Do we really want to move on? Are we ready to get what we need in life?

It is far easier to go to bat for others; it is perhaps the greatest challenge of adulthood to know truly who we are and what we need, and then to really and truly go to bat for ourselves! Ready?

STRATEGIES

1 Rehearse

In order to Evolve—which is to say, remain unprovoked, not just be able to recover from a provocation—we must be ready for the triggers that hook us. We prepare ourselves by recognizing our predictable triggers, then Rehearsing our response.

•We start by using candid, calm observation to identify the issues or people that tend to trigger us, and to recognize our own typical reaction.

• Next we prepare four or five "ready lines" to pull out and use at these predictable trigger moments. The purpose of these "ready lines" is to keep us calm, so we remain the person we want to be.

• Then we Rehearse these specific words and actions so that we're ready to use them when a trigger moment occurs.

Our rehearsed lines defuse the triggers, enabling us to stay smooth, rather than become defensive, angry, hurt, or demanding. Plan ahead, prepare, rehearse: these are the core components of Evolve. Once we master them, we find ourselves living more easily, since we are much less likely to be caught off guard.

TIP

I find that when people do not have rehearsed words and phrases on tap, they do not make the changes they seek to make. It's just too hard come up with these words in the heat of the moment. But when they pause and take time to prepare and rehearse some "ready lines," they find they can hang on to their composure.

Here's How it Works

▶ Jessica notices that she is easily provoked by Colleen, a colleague she encounters once a year at the company retreat.

Observe: Jessica takes the time to really Observe what it is about being with Colleen that sets her off. She sees that Colleen has a habit of asking deep, prying questions, which Jessica finds too personal and revealing, in front of other colleagues. This year, instead of brushing off her feelings and telling herself not to be so sensitive, Jessica decides to listen to herself. She acknowledges, "I do not like sharing personal information with work colleagues. It makes me feel vulnerable."

Visualize: Rather than hope or assume that Colleen won't ask personal questions this year, Jessica prepares. She Visualizes what she wants: to stay calm, friendly, and open, yet not reveal overly personal information that makes her feel vulnerable.

Evolve: Jessica Rehearses ahead of time a few lines that will enable her to keep the conversation at a comfortable level. In response to any questions about a traumatic car accident she was in, her sister, or her stepmother, Jessica is prepared to say:

- Oh my, wouldn't that be another hour's conversation. Tell me, what have you been up to?

- Hmmm, what a topic. Who saw a great movie this year?

- Family—what can I say? So what was your favorite restaurant when you were in New York?

▶ Stuart's son, Ray, now twenty-three, struggles with addiction. Ray burns through his money, then asks Stuart for more. Stuart wants to be a helpful parent, yet is no longer willing to feel complicit in supporting Ray's drug expenses—a feeling that triggers intense feelings of regret, anger at being used, hurt, and confusion.

Evolve: Stuart decides to Evolve into a parent who can decide what he invests in, on his own terms. While Stuart is never sure just when he will hear from Ray, he knows Ray will call again sometime. So Stuart rehearses a response that will help him feel ready, steady, and mature:

"Ray, it sounds like you need help. I have put money in a health care spending account for you. It will cover some medical expenses, including counseling or rehab. It matters to me that you get what you need."

2 | Swim in Your Own Lane

This strategy inoculates you against rescuing others whom you consider less fortunate than yourself—a very provocative challenge. It recognizes that we are all different, with different capacities, inherent gifts, and learned skills that cause us to "swim" through life at different speeds and paces than other people we know, even others in our own family, school, or work groups.

When we Swim in Our Own Lane, we recognize that every person has their own lane and swims at the pace they choose or are capable of, to the best of their ability. Sadly, we sometimes notice that those we love, or even those we depend on, are floundering or even drowning in their lane. This is very distracting and potentially fatal for us if we leave our own lane to jump in and "rescue" them. It is extremely difficult NOT to do this; how can we look the other way? Yet how can we reach our own truest potential if we spend a great portion of our life swimming in someone else's lane?

Swimming in our own lane does not mean we ignore others who are floundering. We stay in our lane and toss them a life-ring; we send in a lifeguard (a doctor or therapist); we recommend strategies we have learned; we offer tips, hope, help, and guidance; we cheer, we cry, we encourage; but we do not leave our lane permanently. We may, at times, hop out of our lane, hop into someone else's, and give them a boost. We know this is the right amount of helping if they start moving forward again—and if we don't start to drown along with them.

Troubling signs:

- The other keeps floundering after we have left our own lane and is still scrambling in her lane after an extended period of time.

- We do not feel proud or fulfilled by our rescue effort, but rather exhausted, used up, weak, resentful or vulnerable.

We know we are giving the right amount when we are still whole, still have an "I" left. We have given too much if there are now two victims or we find ourselves being dragged underwater too. These are signals that the other person needs someone else to help him this time. Perhaps we can point him in that direction, while we live the life we are intended to live.

The best way to ensure that we move forward in our life, as we are meant to do, is to live up to our fullest potential in our lane, while offering the right amount of encouragement and assistance to others so they live up to their highest potential in their own lanes. That way we can all swim to our fullest potential. It is important to remember that we did not cause these differences, we cannot always control these differences, and it is up to each of us to swim to our very best in our lane.

> ### Here's How it Works

▶ Billy's brother, Rob, is severely developmentally delayed. He is unable to attend regular schooling. Billy, on the other hand, is academically gifted and headed to a top college. Haunted, he sometimes wonders, "Is it okay to leave Rob at home while I go away to school? Is that selfish, or will that gap expose Rob's limitations even further?"

Billy recognizes that he and his brother have two very different life lanes, and probably always will. Billy has a potential to reach and so does Rob. It would not be right for Billy to under-hit his potential, or for Rob to under-hit his. Both need to encourage the other to be the best person he can be.

▶ Michelle's daughter, Leigh, a college freshman, is struggling with adjusting to her new roommate, environment, classes, and college life in general. She calls Michelle several times a day at the office to complain about how difficult these adjustments are. Michelle struggles over whether to interrupt her work to take these calls every time.

Michelle sympathizes with her daughter's adjustment difficulties but understands that part of becoming an adult is dealing with your own challenges. She decides to hold off calling Leigh back until she is free in the evening. When she does this she finds that the crisis has passed. Over time, Leigh begins to call less and less during the day.

Michelle also realizes that answering every call suggests that Leigh cannot handle things—the very opposite of the message Michelle wants to convey! Michelle decides to stop leaping out of her own lane for each call, but rather to pause, suggest that Leigh find a few resources to help her solve her own problem, and encourage Leigh to be strong. In this way Michelle shifts from a Rescuer to a mother who encourages her daughter to be the best Leigh she can be.

3 Throw Them a Bone

This strategy inoculates you against remaining the victim of very power-hungry people. You will notice that some people really seem to require ego stroking, kudos, validation, attention, and so on. When we are poised, mature, and evolved, we can give them a dose of this attention in order to keep our own life moving in the direction we choose. We are NOT acquiescing or sucking up . . . we are skillfully paying attention to someone's need, human flaw, Skill Gap, or lack of evolution, and having compassion for it. Throwing Them a Bone recognizes that giving just a little of whatever the person seems so bent on having might help us focus our energy where we want it most. This strategy does not mean giving in; it is a strategic way to move forward from a position of greater vision.

> ### Here's How it Works

▶ Brianna works with an egotistical, insecure partner who seems to reject every original thought she presents. He seems intent on being "the one" who has ideas, is right, is the "winner," while squelching her creative potential.

Having Moved Back from the emotional sting of this behavior, Brianna Observes that her coworker really seems to need lots of kudos, and she Visualizes a workplace where her ideas are considered, legitimized, and adopted. Brianna is ready to float new ideas past her coworker. She approaches him this way:

"Bill. Please put your eagle eye on this idea. With your skillful input, this concept I am working on can take hold. Thank you for giving it your golden touch. I look forward to moving this up the chain together."

▶ Cathy works in a law firm with Dave, an attorney who repeatedly chastises her for not keeping him "informed, updated, and briefed." She is at her wits' end, because every time she requests a meeting to align with Dave, he is "too busy" and says her request is "not important."

Move Back: Cathy Moves Back from her emotional confusion and Observes that Dave has a need to feel informed but no intent to prioritize a meeting with her.

Visualize: She Visualizes smooth interactions between them in which he is grateful for her briefings. Now she handles him like this:

Each morning, Cathy casually drops by Dave's office door, holding briefing summaries. She pauses and says, "Good morning, Dave. I have reports here whenever you want them. Just want to touch base and keep you updated. Is there anything you need from me today?"

Cathy is amazed to find that Dave turns out not to actually need anything from her other than giving him the sense that she is informing him and not keeping information from him. She has thrown him a bone.

4 | Be Entertained

Here is another booster shot against victimization, in this case by people who are mean, nasty, or behaving badly. When we Evolve, we are no longer flabbergasted or hurt by people and events. We learn to Be Entertained. We see things from a healthy emotional distance, with a candid perspective, and through the lens of emotional mastery. Instead of being shocked, we are prepared. We show up to whatever freak show or drama is going on holding virtual popcorn, prepared to observe events as they unfold. In fact we are ready to rank the drama on an entertainment scale of one to ten. Sometimes we even entertain ourselves!

Here's How it Works

▶ Sanjay is separating from his wife of twenty-three years, who has grown increasingly hostile, unpredictable, and mean toward him. She is often hysterical, crying and ranting, "Why have you ruined my life? You are selfish and cruel! You will be hated by everyone for leaving me, including our children!"

Move Back and Observe: Understandably, Sanjay needs to gain a healthy emotional distance from her actions and words. He is not cruel; he wishes her no harm. He simply needs to move on in his life without feeling trapped in a marriage that does not feed him in any way. He Moves Back and Observes her carefully and scientifically enough to know that she can be unpredictable and that he needs to always be prepared for her worst to show up.

Visualize: He Visualizes himself remaining calm no matter what verbal projectiles she hurls at him.

Evolve: Sanjay is learning to Be Entertained, rather than wounded, by her unproductive, off-base comments. He "pops virtual popcorn" when he encounters his wife and prepares himself for a tirade. When it occurs, he thinks to himself, "And there it is!" He rates it candidly: "Wow, a 9.9 today! She is really worked up." Or "Hmmm, a 3.8. She must be in a good mood for some reason."

Sanjay has evolved from someone who needed his wife to be civil—a need that could not be met anytime soon. He is now someone who takes care of himself no matter what she throws his way. So his response to her tirade is, "I see we are not talking; instead there is screaming. I will return when we can have a conversation."

► Celine is a fourth-grader whose teacher this year is a real screamer. Celine is brought into counseling for night sweats, stomach cramps every day before school, and a drop in grades. Her mother explains that this is not like Celine; she was a top student last year and enjoyed going to school. Celine says she is "terrified" of her teacher, who yells, belittles, and insults, regularly reducing her students to tears. Celine's mother has complained to the school administration, but she feels her daughter needs help now, in case a decision to remove this teacher drags on. Celine needs tools to use immediately!

Be Entertained: Celine has had no other symptoms of distress or anxiety. Her problem is situational. In this case, it is worth trying tools, as opposed to medication. Celine will learn to find Mrs. K. entertaining.

Each day, Celine prepares for school by observing to herself, "Mrs. K. is a screamer"—not a housecat. Celine reminds herself that Mrs. K. yells at everyone. Celine is not causing it, nor can she control it, but she can be okay with it!

Once Celine is mentally prepared for Mrs. K.'s outbursts, they do not catch her off guard. Every day, she is ready to pop the virtual popcorn and rate the "movie." Will it be a 9.9 (a blowout)? Or a mild 4.2 today? Will she yell at Rodney, Sasha, or the whole class? Will she yell once today or ten times? Celine repeats to herself, "I would really prefer a calmer teacher. I hope I have one next year. This year, I really have a screamer."

Note that Celine does not participate in gossip; she does not act disrespectfully to the teacher's face. But she does call it like it is—the essential truth-facing strategy Just the Facts, from Step 2—and Categorize It. This allows Celine to shift from being a naïve, victimized "nice girl" to a smart girl who is prepared to face the world as it is.

BUT WAIT!

Isn't Be Entertained a recipe for tolerating abuse?

No! No one should ever tolerate abuse. Notice that Sanjay leaves and only returns when he is treated fairly. It is just for the moment, to maintain his composure and mental well-being in the face of his wife's tirade, that he shifts from being wounded to being entertained, noting his ability to achieve emotional distance from her words.

Note also that Celine's mother is working to have this teacher removed. Verbal abuse can have real, lasting negative consequences and must be addressed. Neither Sanjay nor Celine should remain in their current circumstances indefinitely. Be Entertained is a real-time strategy for handling a difficult person in the moment without feeling victimized.

Physical abuse is another matter entirely. If you are ever being physically hurt or threatened, you get away. Once your physical safety is ensured, you can begin to think through what your strategy for moving forward in life needs to be.

5   What Does the Queen/King Need?

As I've explained, it is far more productive to view stuck points in life in terms of a Skill Gap rather than as an enduring personal failing. When we hit a roadblock, we look for skills, tools, resources, references, and people to help us "skill through" the challenge. A helpful strategy that encourages you to Evolve from a frantic intern or adolescent trying desperately to please others into a mature adult who is clear about her or his own worth is to ask yourself, "What Does the Queen/King Need?"

In this strategy, we adopt the posture of a mature executive or leader who needs outside assistance in order to be great. "Get my people!" we exclaim when we are stuck. "Who can help me? Who can I surround myself with? Where are my resources?!" translates into "What tools, technology, classes, phone numbers, and so on might I need to be more successful here?"

The Queen and King are aware of their worth; aware of the challenges that face them; and smart enough to know they need resources to thrive. They do not go it alone, nor do they expect to know it all. They create a court around them that supplies regular briefings, information, and tools that help them remain successful. We, too, can become the Kings and Queens of our lives. Ask yourself what the Queen/King needs to be successful in any given situation—and see what happens.

Here's How it Works

▶ Julie was recently promoted. She feels overwhelmed with new tasks for which she has had little training or preparation. She is afraid people will discover she doesn't know enough to do this new job, yet she is aware she was promoted for a reason. She Looks Ahead, sees herself adapting fully into this role, and becomes the Queen. She asks, "What does the Queen need to be successful?"

> Julie identifies a list of skills, informational briefings, trainings, and on-ramping meetings she will request. She does not blame or judge herself for her lack of knowledge; she sees it as a Skill Gap that the Queen must address right away. Nor does she wait for others to read her mind and identify her needs. She is mature and can obtain what she needs herself.

▶ Donna is responsible for organizing a huge event: the mayor's election party. She has thrown events before for her family and is a friend of the mayor, but this event exceeds anything she has ever taken on. She Moves Back, Finds Her Center, recognizes her Skill Gap (she is not a professional party planner), Visualizes a wonderful event, and becomes the Queen.

> Donna contacts the mayor's office and offers three options for the event: a simple home-style reception; a welcoming at a local restaurant for which she would need to appoint a handful of assistants; or an extensive gala at the Convention Center for which Donna would hire an event planner and oversee that person's work. In all cases, Donna has made sure her needs will be met.

6 | Sprinkle Disappointment

You cannot remain an adult without sprinkling a little disappointment around you. At times, you will even need to throw a grenade. People who repeatedly struggle with not wanting to hurt others will wind up struggling to meet their own needs adequately. It is simply not possible to take care of your own needs consistently and well without occasionally letting others down—saying no, disappointing them, even sometimes really hurting them. Just remember that other people are resilient too! They can become adults and handle the disappointment just fine, if you let them.

Sprinkle Disappointment comes into play when we realize we need something that pits us against someone else's need. For example, you need rest, but your children want to go to the mall. You need a day off, but your boss begs you to come in to work on an urgent assignment. You want to stay home for Hanukah, but your mother wants you to join her at your brother's. Will you find a way to get your needs met? Or will you remain the victim who takes care of everyone else's needs and then feels resentment, sadness, fatigue, or regret?

TIP

Resentment is the very first cue that we are not meeting our own needs! Watch for it. Others don't make us resentful. We allow it to happen by not meeting our own needs well enough. Consult your Resent-O-Meter, and at the first sign of resentment, stop! Move Back; Pause; Observe, "What is going on for me? What is it I really want?" and Visualize: "Is there a way to get my needs met here?" Now Evolve by Sprinkling a Little Disappointment.

Here's How it Works

▶ You have put in a full week at work. It is 4:30 on Friday afternoon, and you are looking forward to the weekend. As you pack up your things, your coworker pops his head in and says, "Jolene! Thank goodness you are still here. I really need your help on the Simons assignment. It's due first thing Monday morning. You can whip it out in no time."

You feel yourself becoming hot in the face, provoked, tense. You are aware that this is the cue that you are feeling triggered.

Move Back: You Pause and say, "Hmmm, hold up. Let me look at something. I'll come find you." This buys you time.

Observe: If you say "no" you will seem unhelpful. You like being the hero! The one who gets it done, no matter what! Yet you also Observe that you are unhappy being the one who stays until 10:00 PM on Friday night while others go home. At the same time, you know your coworker has a wedding to attend this weekend. Your saying no will mean a long, hard weekend for him.

Evolve: You ask yourself, "What does the Queen need right now?" She needs some rest! You recognize that you did not cause or create this problem. Some days you have problems of your own to face, but today this is his problem, not yours. It stinks to be him. His swimming lane is a hard one this weekend.

Rehearse and Sprinkle Disappointment: Since you want to take care of your own needs in a mature way, you decide to compose a response that honors your needs and also reflects well on you. You Rehearse your words, preparing to Sprinkle Disappointment. Then you walk to your coworker's office and say, "I am so sorry. I have an obligation that I cannot break. I will do my fair share first thing Monday morning. You know I love to help when I can. Today, I can't. Good luck." (Ouch. You can feel the bomb going off over there, right in front of him. So be careful—don't look too closely.)

It truly stinks to be him right now. But remember: he is an adult. What you have learned is that you must stop making it stink to be you every Friday! You leave the office knowing that this was not easy, and you have left him in the lurch. However, disappointing him was an important step for you in becoming the adult, not remaining the victim. You wish him well.

▶ Your ten-year-old daughter, Stacy, wants to play field hockey this spring. It's expensive. It's time-consuming. And time is tight. This is a particularly demanding season, since her two next older brothers are committed to travel sports, and her oldest brother is preparing to leave for college. You agreed as a family that Stacy would take the season off so that you could focus on these other activities until next year, when it will be her turn.

Stacy has forgotten that this was the decision. She comes home from school all excited: "Mom! Field hockey looks like fun! I want to play!" You feel the tug of guilt and sadness. Is it right or fair to tell her no? You start to doubt your decision. Yet you also know how much it will burden you and the family if you over-commit. You feel nauseated and sad—and that is your trigger-cue.

Move Back and Observe: What is in everyone's best interests this year? You have learned that if your family takes on too many events at one time, you will tank physically and emotionally. You realize that doing so would position you for a very tough, unrewarding spring, and that has consequences for everyone. So you choose to Check the Guilt.

Visualize: You Visualize something very different for yourself this year. You recall having committed to being happier, stronger, more easygoing, and more present to your family than last year's shrieking, perpetually late, resentful mother. You realize you need to Thrive Alongside, even if it means taking turns.

Sprinkle Disappointment: "Stacy, this is not your year for field hockey. Next year, honey. Right now, you can make time each day to practice drills in the back yard." You realize being an evolved adult is not easy, but it is important to the whole family that you be mature—not drained and resentful from giving beyond what you have to give.

TIP

Don't forget that your trigger response—the emotion or physical sensation you have when you feel hurt, attacked, criticized, or surprised—is unique to you. Even behavior that we all agree is provocative will trigger each of us differently. We go to different "hurt places" because we all have different wounds.

Your trigger response is your jewel, because it can reveal precisely what you need to give yourself (the 180-Degree Opposite of that hurt) in order to Evolve.

• For example, when Tatia is under pressure, she worries that she will fail and blames her boss for being intimidating. Curiously, this same boss makes Timon feel inspired, while Gregory is angered by the burden the boss heaps on him.

Each response is a lesson specific to the one who has it.

• Tatia needs to believe in herself and to figure out what she needs to succeed.

• Timon is not triggered by this boss; he enjoys the challenge, and that's fine.

• Gregory needs to prioritize some down time, to honor his need to relax and recover from the challenges of the day.

Becoming an adult is all about learning how to heal your wounds so that you are less susceptible to painful triggers. Pay attention to your trigger response. It is your ticket to evolution.

YOUR TURN

think

Think back over the past week to a situation in which you felt surprised, shocked, hurt, ignored, or had some other reaction that you do not enjoy. Describe what happened.

....

reflect

Now describe what you felt.

....

correct

Which Evolve strategy(ies) could you have used to handle it differently?

Rehearse
Swim in Your Own Lane
Throw Them a Bone
Be Entertained
What Does the Queen/King Need?
Sprinkle Disappointment

....

imagine

How might it have gone if you had used these strategies?

....

take action

Pick one strategy that you will use this week. Describe when you plan to use it.

conclusion

CONCLUSION: START MY DAY HAPPY, END MY DAY HAPPY

Your end goal in MOVE Forward is to have the life you want to have, to the best of your ability, no matter what fate throws at you. Challenges are hurdles but need not become permanent roadblocks when we see that we are resilient; when we seek alternative avenues; and when we continue to acquire new skills to map a way around or through each new challenge. We may encounter a temporary setback, yet stay resolved to find a new route forward. When we view the tough patches of our lives as indicating Skill Gaps, not personal defects, we are more likely to be kind to ourselves as we rise to meet these challenges. We keep in mind that we are Good Enough AND Growing.

Once people in my workshops have learned the four MOVE Forward steps, they generally have a few remaining questions:

▶ Do I need to use the strategies and steps in order?

Not necessarily, although Move Back is certainly rule number one for anyone seeking to remain calm in a highly charged situation. Your first response is always to Move Back, Pause, and not do what you've been doing: your usual reaction.

After that, most people do find that the order of the steps as presented here, M–O–V–E, is very useful. If all you do is begin with a strategy from Move Back, you're already in good shape. Once you can really move back and pause, you're ready to Observe and start asking: what's really going on here? What's my interpretation? And what do I need? What's advisable for me now? When you get good at observing—wonderful.

Your next goal is to clearly Visualize what you want, in order to make it happen. And then you reach the point when you're ready to Evolve and no longer find yourself caught off guard all the time.

You are absolutely not bound by this order, however. You can pick and choose strategies as you like (see the next question).

▶ There are a lot of strategies in this workbook! Am I supposed to remember them all?

There are a lot, yes! And no, you do not have to memorize all of them to begin experiencing real change right away. A good start is to pick one that really speaks to you or seems really useful right now—and stick with it. Use it, over and over and over. Get really good at it! See how it changes things in your life. If you notice that it is not enough, it is time to Skill Up further. Take time to pause, pick up this workbook, and find another strategy to move you forward.

▶ Supposing these tools are not enough? How can I tell whether I need help from a professional counselor?

There are generally two guidelines indicating that it is time to seek professional help.

● First: if you are unable to perform your usual daily functions (waking, getting dressed, eating well, sleeping normally, going to work or tending to your regular tasks), this is a sign that you need outside help, now. To delay is to risk lowering the quality of your life, damaging your health, or jeopardizing important relationships or income.

● Second: frustration. If you have tried these strategies (or any other self-help techniques) on your own, yet your problem remains unresolved, an outside eye from a trained expert can often give you traction much more quickly and effectively.

▶ Can you help me? Are you available for consultation?

I am available to help, and I enjoy it. I provide counseling, coaching, seminars, and workshops in person, via web, by phone, and by Skype. If you feel you or someone you know might benefit from working with me, by all means contact me. Call me at my office (302) 543-6296, or send an email to Lani@LNZconsulting.com. I'll tailor these tools to your specific situation to help you experience important changes.

▶ How do I know if I need medication? Or if someone I love needs it?

The decision to medicate is not to be made lightly. You should seek expert help from a qualified, licensed medical practitioner. The best indicators that you may be a candidate for medication are:

- You are suicidal;

- You cannot move through your daily tasks; or

- You have tried counseling alone and seen little to no benefit.

Medications, properly prescribed, may relieve your symptoms enough to enable you to develop the skills and strategies you need to cope. Medication without new strategies only masks your problems. It will not solve them. Make sure you acquire real tools for handling your life!

▶ Will I ever be good at coping? Will I ever really change?

Another great question. Its underlying implication is, "I doubt I can change. I have tried before and I am pretty stuck with this current problem or in my current ways." In such a case, it's quite understandable that you would be doubtful. Here is what I know.

- In order to change, you must decide to change.

- Then you must dedicate yourself to new goals, with discipline.

- Then you must put your goals into action by practicing new skills and tweaking them as needed, again and again over time.

DECIDE, DEDICATE, PRACTICE, ACHIEVE

This is the recipe for success. If you decide to change, try a strategy once or twice, and then find yourself reverting to old habits or reacting to old triggers, you may feel like giving up. But remember: Decide, dedicate, practice, achieve. That's how we get results in anything.

▶ Will my life run smoothly if I develop these strategies?

Great question. Your life will never be free of road bumps. That would not be living! To live is to encounter challenge. So the goal is not to have a life with no problems. The goal is to be better prepared, so that your problems remain road bumps, not roadblocks. When you achieve this goal you will be more apt to respond to road bumps—even huge ones—with grace, dignity, and composure.

▶   How long does it take to Evolve?

I do not have a crystal ball. But here is a rule of thumb from the field of behavior change.

- Try a new goal behavior seven times: it starts to become familiar.

- Repeat it for seven weeks: it starts to become habit.

- Sustain it for seven months: it starts to become the new you.

- Voilà! You have evolved!

Your Last Strategy: Damn Adequate!

What is the result of mastering all these steps and strategies? Believing once and for all that you are Damn Adequate!

Damn Adequate is the evolved counterpart of Good Enough AND Growing. Knowing you are Damn Adequate means you have evolved to a place where you understand you are human, you accept that you have gifts and limitations, you seek skills and resources when you get stuck (rather than wallow in self-punishment), and you are proud of the person you have become . . . you smile inside and say, "I am Damn Adequate!"

- You do not engage in conversations you do not want to have.

- You do not take on activities you hate (except when you choose to endure them for a time for the sake of a greater reward).

- You convey to the world that you are fine with yourself and your choices; you have no need to be either boastful or self-deprecating.

- The proverbial "suggestion box" on your chest is closed. You are not open to unsolicited criticisms.

- You can pick and choose when you will engage in self-reflection, with whom, on what days, in what places, when you are in what kind of mood. You are not a project for others to control.

- You have little time anymore for petty comparisons; you are living the life you want. If there is something you feel you want more of, you go to work making it happen.

Damn Adequate is how you feel when you are in charge of your self-discovery process, which proceeds at the pace that works best for you and in a way that you believe will enable you to grow. And you will grow, because you have discovered that you can change. Life is more rewarding. You begin to see new tools and resources all around you.

No longer do you feel the need to defend, cover up, hope, compare, wish, wait, or perfect yourself. When you see that hook slide out—the one you used to get hung up on and thrash around helplessly—you no longer get caught on it; you sidestep around it.

Here's How it Works

▶ You were an overachiever who worked relentlessly to earn people's praise, even though it wasn't necessary. But you have evolved, and you no longer need it. You know now that you are Damn Adequate.

> Someone at work tries to throw a hook into you: "Shouldn't you be more involved in this project? What will the boss think of your leaving on time today?"

> You respond, "I gave 110 percent today. Lou can handle this one. He does a great job."

> You walk away proud to know you are a Damn Adequate employee who does not have to prove himself daily. You can even allow others to shine.

▶ You work overnight shifts several times a year and have candidly assessed that they take a toll on you. After a long week of overnight shifts, you need a few days off to recover, or else your health and sanity are in jeopardy. You cannot control when these shifts are assigned to you, so sometimes you have to Sprinkle Disappointment on family functions in order to take care of yourself.

> You saw these shifts coming just before Easter week and let the family know you would see them two weeks after Easter but would stay at home and rest on Easter weekend.

Your sister, caught up in the family guilt drama, calls two days before Easter and pleads, "Can't you come home? Mom will be devastated if you are not here for Easter Sunday!" You recognize that tug, you are prepared for it, and you respond graciously, "And I will really miss her and you! If I could change the master schedule, I would. Have a great holiday and enjoy a slice of carrot cake for me!"

You are also prepared in case your sister persists: "But Mom will be miserable! Isn't there something you can do?!" You Thank Her Forward and advocate for yourself directly: "Sis, I'm doing what I need to do. I hope you can understand. I give what I can, and I give from the heart. I'll call you all on Sunday, and I'll see you in two weeks. Take care, and thanks for understanding."

You hang up the phone proud of yourself, knowing you are not a perfect son or person, but that you are Damn Adequate in showing your care for others.

▶ You had a habit of comparing yourself to other women. They always seemed prettier, thinner, happier . . . on and on.

You have just recently begun working hard to commit to seeing yourself as Good Enough AND Growing. You talk nicely to yourself, encourage yourself, and work out more often.

After only three weeks, a formal event comes up on the calendar. You begin to feel the old tug: "I haven't had enough time! I'm not thin enough! I have more weight to lose!"

You remember Damn Adequate and stop! You look at yourself in the mirror and say, "You are fabulous. You look lovely." You stand tall as you head to the event, Damn Adequate!

▶ You have prepared an important presentation. All eyes will be on you. You have worked months to get it ready, poring over each word. It's show time. You look down and notice two pages missing. How could this happen?! You feel that surge of panic. You are tempted to berate yourself and your secretary, or just run!

You calm down, smile, and find your sense that you are Damn Adequate. You remember that you are human, and your audience is too. Mistakes happen, the world goes on, you have much to offer.

You retain your sense of being human as you begin speaking: "Ladies and gentleman, we have a wonderful presentation for you. You will gain a solid overview of our product. I just noticed that pages 7 and 8 are missing in this version, but I will walk you through the content of those pages. Anyone who wants copies of these two pages, just let us know, and we'll see to it that you receive the complete copy. Shall we begin?"

When you are Damn Adequate, your life is smooth. It is good now, AND it will keep getting better. We are not expecting to feel better when we grow; we are not waiting to feel happy when things change. We are evolved enough to be happy right now—even as we are human and continue growing. A mature, evolved self is poised for a life of continuous adaptation and improvement. We enjoy the ride, bumps and all.

ACKNOWLEDGMENTS

Three people were directly involved in the creation of this workbook. I want to thank Cindy Heck for her instructional writing expertise—she took the lead in organizing these concepts into a workbook. She has tremendous technical skill. Cindy connected me with Alexandra Tornek, who provided the marvelous layout and design. And Stephanie Golden provided the professional consultation on writing, flow, structure, and readability. I truly had the "A-Team" working with me!

I also want to thank my "Life Team"—Diane Beneck, Jane Cislo, Charlotte Grabau, Cindy Heck, and Kathy Samworth. We formed this team over a decade ago to help each other maintain our highest life priorities, whatever they happened to be. Thanks to them, my workbook got done while my life got lived.

I also want to acknowledge my family. My husband, George, is terrific, hilarious, and loving. He is way beyond Damn Adequate! And I am grateful to my children, Gian, Tyler, and Talia, for their patience, support, wit, and maturity. I hit the gene jackpot with these three. Thank you to my parents for their love and support, to my in-laws for theirs as well, and to my neighbors, especially Lin and Jan, for pitching in wherever needed. It takes a village, and I am grateful for mine.

ABOUT THE AUTHOR

Dr. Lani Nelson-Zlupko is a therapist, researcher, and consultant with over twenty years of professional experience helping individuals and organizations effectively manage transition. She is on faculty at the University of Pennsylvania and is the founder of LNZ Consulting, providing solution-focused consultation to individuals and organizations seeking to move forward.

Lani has a B.A. from Harvard University, and she received a master's degree in social work and a doctorate in social policy and practice from the University of Pennsylvania. She has led and assisted numerous national and regional research projects, has published in several leading psychology and social work journals, and has trained therapists across the country in best practices.

Lani lives with her husband and three children in Wilmington, Delaware.

Made in the USA
Monee, IL
26 July 2022